BEAUTY
IN A
BROKEN PLACE

The Abbey Theatre

BEAUTY
IN A
BROKEN PLACE

COLM TÓIBÍN

THE LILLIPUT PRESS | DUBLIN

First published 2004 by
THE LILLIPUT PRESS
62–63 Sitric Road, Arbour Hill,
Dublin 7, Ireland
www.lilliputpress.ie

A CIP record for this title is available from The British Library.

1 3 5 7 9 10 8 6 4 2

ISBN 1 84351 054 5

Set in 11 on 14 pt Dante
Printed by ColourBooks, Baldoyle, Dublin

The Abbey Theatre and The Lilliput Press gratefully acknowledge financial support from An Chomhairle Ealaíon / The Arts Council of Ireland.

for June Levine and Ivor Browne

abbeyonehundred

In 2004 the Abbey Theatre celebrates one hundred years as Ireland's national theatre.

Both our programmes of on-stage work and ancillary events are particularly exciting and unique to this special year. On stage, the five-season programme has been devised to mark and celebrate the year in a diverse and extensive manner, and coheres around five identifiable themes: *The Abbey and Europe*; *The Abbey and New Writing*; *Summer at the Abbey*; *The Abbey and Ireland* and *The Abbey on Tour*. The five key strands to our programme of events are: *Common Bonds*, *Facing Forward*, *'Author, Author'*, *Marking and Remarking* and our *Abbey Birthday* celebration (27th December 2004). These events are in keeping with our philosophy of artistic and social inclusiveness containing a wide range of community, education and artist development programmes.

The Abbey Theatre will present over thirty productions and hundreds of performances in Ireland and throughout the world in 2004 as it reaches out to over a million people.

I hope you enjoy our production of Colm Tóibín's *Beauty in a Broken Place* as part of *Summer at the Abbey*.

Welcome to **abbey**onehundred.

Ben Barnes
Artistic Director

Beauty in a Broken Place by Colm Tóibín was first performed at the Abbey Theatre, Dublin, on 11th August 2004. Press night was 16th August 2004.

The play is set in 1926.

The performance runs without an interval.

CAST

SEAN O'CASEY	Donal O'Kelly
LADY GREGORY / MRS SHEEHY SKEFFINGTON	Derbhle Crotty
MISS CROWE / MISS CRAIG / MARION / MAUD GONNE MacBRIDE / FIRST WOMAN	Karen Ardiff
MISS DELANY / MRS YEATS / MISS RICHARDS / ANNE / MISS MOONEY / SECOND WOMAN	Caitríona Ní Mhurchú
W.B. YEATS / F.J. McCORMICK / MAN'S VOICE / GARDA MORONEY	Seán Campion
LENNOX ROBINSON / GEORGE O'BRIEN / BARLOW / GARDA GILHOOLEY / MR SHIELDS / BARMAN	Karl Shiels
DIRECTOR	Niall Henry
DESIGNER	Jamie Vartan
LIGHTING DESIGNER	Paul Keogan
SOUND	Eddie Breslin
DRAMATURG	Jocelyn Clarke
VOICE DIRECTOR	Andrea Ainsworth
STAGE DIRECTOR	Audrey Hession
ASSISTANT STAGE MANAGER	Laura Mullan
DIRECTOR OF THE PEACOCK	Ali Curran
CASTING DIRECTOR	Marie Kelly
SET	Abbey Theatre Workshop
COSTUMES	Abbey Theatre Wardrobe Department
PUBLICITY	Gerry Lundberg PR

Please note that the text of the play that appears in this volume may be changed during the rehearsal process and appear in a slightly altered form in performance.

Colm Tóibín *Author*

Colm Tóibín is the author of five novels: *The South* (1990), winner of The Irish Times First Fiction Award; *The Heather Blazing* (1992), winner of the Encore Prize; *The Story of the Night* (1996), winner of the Ferro-Grumley Prize for the best gay novel of the year published in the United States; *The Blackwater Lightship* (1999), shortlisted for the Booker Prize and filmed last year starring Angela Lansbury and Dianne Wiest; and *The Master* (2004). In 1995, he was awarded the E.M. Forster Prize from the American Academy of Arts and Letters, and in 2000 a fellowship at the Center for Scholars and Writers at New York Public Library. His non-fiction includes *Homage to Barcelona* (1990) and *Lady Gregory's Toothbrush* (2002). He is the editor of *The Penguin Book of Irish Fiction* and a regular contributor to *The London Review of Books* and *The New York Review of Books*. He is a member of Aosdána. His work has been translated into twenty-two languages.

Niall Henry *Director*

Niall trained in Paris under Corinne Soum, Maximillion Decroux and Marcel Marceau. Returning to Ireland in 1991 he established Blue Raincoat with Malcolm Hamilton. He has been the company's Artistic Director since its inception and has directed over forty productions for Blue Raincoat in that time. This is the third occasion he has directed for the Abbey Theatre.

Jamie Vartan *Designer*

Jamie Vartan trained at Central Saint Martins School of Art and Design, London. He was awarded an Arts Council Bursary to work at Nottingham Playhouse where he designed several productions. He last collaborated with Niall Henry with designs for *The Playboy of the Western World* at the Peacock Theatre. At the

Abbey Theatre he has also designed *The Playboy of the Western World*, *The Hostage* and *Blackwater Angel* and at the Peacock, *A Little Like Paradise*, *Sour Grapes*, *Making History*, *Doldrum Bay* and *Mrs Warren's Profession* (nominated for the Irish Times/ESB Irish Theatre Best Production Award). He spent three years as designer and artist-in-residence with the David Glass Ensemble on *The Lost Child Trilogy* with residencies in Vietnam, Indonesia, China, the Philippines and Colombia. *The Trilogy* was later presented at the Young Vic. *The Hansel Gretel Machine* (part one of *The Trilogy*) was selected for the 1999 Prague Quadrennial. Designs for opera include *La Traviata* (Malmo), *A Village Romeo and Juliet* (*L'Opera* magazine nomination Best Set and Costume Design 2002) and *Aida* (Cagliari), *Der Zwerg* (Florence and Turin), *La Statira* (Teatro San Carlo, Naples) and currently, *The Queen of Spades* (La Scala, Milan).

Paul Keogan *Lighting Designer*

Born in Dublin, Paul studied drama at Trinity College Dublin and Glasgow University. After graduating he worked for the Project Arts Centre as Production Manager. He designed set and lighting for *The Rite of Spring* (CoisCéim), *Angel/Babel* and *Chair* (Operating Theatre). Other lighting designs include *Lady Macbeth of Mtensk* and *The Silver Tassie* (Opera Ireland), *The Lighthouse* (Opera Theatre Company), *Un Ballo in Maschera* and *The Makropulos Case* (Opera Zuid), and *La Musica* (Siren Productions). Recent work includes *Passades* for Operating Theatre and *Catalyst* for Rex Levitates and The Chinese National Ballet in Beijing. He recently designed the lighting for *Heavenly Bodies* for the Peacock.

Karen Ardiff *Miss Crowe/Miss Craig/Marion/ Maud Gonne MacBride/First Woman*

Karen was born in Dublin and graduated from the Samuel Beckett Centre in Trinity College Dublin. Previous appearances for the Abbey and Peacock Theatres include *Doldrum Bay*, *Love in the Title* (Abbey international tour, for which she won the Irish Times/ESB Best Actress Award), *Caoineadh Airt Uí Laoghaire*, *Cúirt an Mheán Oíche* (Peacock and national tour), *Judas of the Gallarus*, *The Rivals*, *Tarry Flynn* (Abbey and Royal National Theatre), *The Marriage of Figaro*, *The Well of the Saints* (Abbey and Paris tour), *Good Evening, Mr Collins* (Peacock and national tour) and *The Crucible*. Other theatre work includes *Kvetch* (Kilkenny Arts Festival), *How I Learned To Drive* (Lyric, Belfast), *The Cherry Orchard*, *A Month in the Country* and *The Seagull* (Gate Theatre), *The Ashfire* (Pigsback), *The Winter's Tale* and *Coriolanus* (English Shakespeare Company) and *The Importance of Being Earnest* and *Taste* (Gúna Nua). Film and television credits include *Evelyn*, *Sinners*, *This is My Father* and *Ballykissangel* (BBC/RTÉ), *Fergus's Wedding* and *Glenroe* (RTÉ). She has performed in many radio plays for RTÉ, BBC NI and Crazy Dog Radio.

Seán Campion *W.B. Yeats/F.J. McCormick/ Man's Voice/Garda Moroney*

Seán trained at the Focus Theatre, Dublin. Seán previously performed at the Abbey and Peacock Theatres in *Da*, *Tarry Flynn*, *The Importance of Being Earnest*, *Macbeth*, *Big Maggie*, *Rosencrantz and Guildenstern are Dead*, *The Silver Tassie*, *Observe the Sons of Ulster Marching Towards the Somme*, *Good Evening, Mr Collins*, *Hubert Murray's Widow*, *Antigone*, *Calvary/Resurrection* and *Cúirt an Mheán Oíche*. Seán performed in the hugely successful *Stones in His Pockets*, which played in Dublin, Belfast, the West End

London and Broadway and he received an Oliver Award, a Tony Award and an Evening Standard Award Nomination for Best Actor. Other theatre credits include *The Quare Fellow* (Oxford Stage Company), *Winners/Interior* (Young Vic), *Translations* and *Bent* (Red Kettle Theatre Company), *Equus* and *Canaries* (Gaiety Theatre), *Mutabilitie* (Royal National Theatre), *A Moon for the Misbegotten* (Dubbeljoint Theatre Company), *Miss Julie* (Everyman Palace), *Poor Superman* (Muted Cupid Theatre Company), *The Mayor of Casterbridge* (Storytellers Theatre Company), and *Waiting for Godot*. Film and television credits include *Glenroe* and *Fair City* (RTÉ), *Echoes* (Channel 4), *Most Important* (Parzival Productions), *Goldfish Memory, The Blackwater Lightship* and *Timbuktu*.

Derbhle Crotty *Lady Gregory/Mrs Sheehy Skeffington*

Derbhle's work at the Abbey and Peacock Theatres includes *The Plough and the Stars, Bailegangaire, Portia Coughlan* (Royal Court Co-production), *The Well of the Saints* (Edinburgh Festival and Perth), *The Mai* and *Katie Roche*. Other theatre work includes *Dancing at Lughnasa* (Gate Theatre), *The Playboy of the Western World, Summerfolk* and *The Merchant of Venice* (Royal National Theatre), *The Weir* (Royal Court on tour), *Little Eyolf, Camino Real* and *Hamlet* (Royal Shakespeare Company), *Playing the Wife* (Chichester), *Miss Julie* (Vesuvius), *Measure for Measure* (Gallowglas), and *Sive, Gaslight* and *The Good Father* (Druid Theatre Company). Film and television credits include *Inside I'm Dancing, The Merchant of Venice, Poorhouse, Gold in the Streets, Samhain* and *Any Time Now*. Radio credits include *The Weight of Water* and *St Patrick's Daughter* (BBC Woman's Hour), *Quinn, Bailegangaire, Portia Coughlan, The Gospels of Aughamore* and *King Lear* (RTÉ Radio 1).

Caitríona Ní Mhurchú *Miss Delany/Mrs Yeats/ Miss Richards/Anne/Miss Mooney/Second Woman*

Caitríona trained at the Gaiety School of Acting. Her last appearance at the Abbey and Peacock Theatres was as Verona in *Ariel*. Other theatre work includes *Kandachime* with Torifune Butoh Sha (Samuel Beckett Theatre), Queen Elizabeth in *Richard III* (Theatreworks), Innes in *Innes de Castro* (Theatre Space), Trish in *Ding Dong* (Cork Opera House), Woman from Rathmines in Stephen Rea's version of *The Plough and the Stars* (Gaiety Theatre), Sorcha in *Caoineadh Airt Uí Laoghaire* (Peacock Theatre), Mrs Cheverley in *An Ideal Husband* (Andrews Lane Theatre), Máire in *Dún na mBan Trí Thine* (Amharclann de hÍde). Film and television credits include *Proof*, *Fair City* and *On Home Ground* (RTÉ), *Trí Scéal* (TG4), *Ballykissangel* (BBC/RTÉ), *The Longest Ditch*, *Kaos*, *Countess Cathleen*, *Mystic Knights*, *My Dinner with Oswald*, *An Turas*, *Sun Moon and Stars* and *Misteach Bhaile Átha Cliath*. Caitríona also writes, directs and voices cartoons for TG4, including *Spongebob Squarepants*, *The Muppets* and *Scooby Doo*.

Donal O'Kelly *Sean O'Casey*

Donal O'Kelly is well known both as an actor and as a writer. His solo play *Catalpa* won a Scotsman Fringe First Award in Edinburgh, shared the Critics' Prize for Best Event at the Melbourne International Festival and played to high acclaim in Washington, Toronto, Chicago, London, Copenhagen and Paris as well as all over Ireland. His solo play *Bat the Father Rabbit the Son* was an acclaimed hit in the Dublin and Edinburgh Festivals and in New York. Both it and *Catalpa* were also broadcast on RTÉ Radio. His latest solo play, *Jimmy Joyced!*, about James Joyce in 1904, opened this summer and tours Ireland this autumn. Stage roles include

Lucky in Walter Asmus' Gate Theatre production of *Waiting for Godot* (World Stage Festival, Toronto), the solo play *Act Without Words I* in the Gate Theatre's Beckett Festival at the Lincoln Center New York, Joxer in *Juno and the Paycock* and Trinculo in *The Tempest* (Abbey Theatre), and a tour of *Baricco's 1900 – the Pianist on the Ocean* (Civic). He also wrote, directed and performed in *The Hand* for the Dublin Theatre Festival 2002. On screen he starred as Bimbo in Roddy Doyle's *The Van.* Other film and television credits include *Spin the Bottle, I Went Down, The Last Bus Home, Hard Shoulder, Stephen, The Marriage* and *Paths to Freedom.*

Karl Shiels *Lennox Robinson/George O'Brien/Barlow/Garda Gilhooley/Mr Shields/Barman*

Karl trained at the Gaiety School of Acting. Previous work for the Abbey and Peacock Theatres includes *Duck, Henry IV, Barbaric Comedies, At Swim-Two-Birds* and *Twenty Grand.* Other theatre credits include *Salomé, Comedians, Howie the Rookie, Greek, Obituary, Fully Recovered, The Spanish Tragedy, Muller's Medea, Early Morning, Quartet, This Lime Tree Bower, The Duchess of Malfi, Fireraisers, As Is, Hamlet* and *Massacre at Paris.* Film and television credits include *Batman Begins, Capital Letters, Intermission, Spin the Bottle, Veronica Guerin, Mystics, Virtues of a Sinner, Meeting Che Guevera, Clubbing, Freaky Deaky 10/1, Daybreak, Getting Close, Any Time Now, On Home Ground, Doctors, Attachments* and *Private Lives.* Directing credits include *Butterflies, Breakfast with Versace, Conversations with a Cupboard Man, Within 24 Hours, Another 24 Hours, 24 Hours of Dance, Slaughter* and *Ladies and Gents* (Semper Fi [Ireland]), *The Pitchfork Disney* and *Fallen* (Raw Image), *Laughing till I Die* (Qumavus), and *Three Tall Women* and the forthcoming *Topdog Underdog* (Tall Tales). Karl is Artistic Director of Semper Fi (Ireland).

abbeyonehundred sponsors

The Abbey Theatre gratefully acknowledges the following for their generous support of **abbey**onehundred.

The Arts Council

Department of Arts, Sport and Tourism

Department of Education and Science

Dermot F. Desmond

Moya Doherty

Lew Glucksman and Loretta Brennan Glucksman

The Ireland Funds

John McColgan

Bernard McNamara

The National Lottery

Denis O'Brien

Bord Gáis

Maurice Cassidy

Gaiety Theatre

The Heritage Council

Today FM

Wagamama

abbeytheatre

abbey theatre staff

BOARD
Eithne Healy - Chairman
Loretta Brennan Glucksman
Eugene Downes
Bernard Farrell
John McColgan
Pauline Morrison
Niall O'Brien
John O'Mahony
Michael J. Somers

ARTISTIC DIRECTOR
Ben Barnes

MANAGING DIRECTOR
Brian Jackson

EXECUTIVE OFFICE
Orla Mulligan

ABBEYONEHUNDRED
Anne Marie Kane
Sharon Murphy
Jennie Scanlon

ABBEY PLAYERS
Des Cave
Clive Geraghty

ARCHIVE
Mairéad Delaney
Aine Kiernan

ASSISTANT STAGE MANAGERS
Marella Boschi
Stephen Dempsey
Pamela McQueen

BOX OFFICE
Des Byrne
Clare Downey
Adam Lawlor

BOX OFFICE CLERKS
Catherine Casey
Anne Marie Doyle
Lorraine Hanna
Iain Mullins
Maureen Robertson
David Windrim

CARPENTERS
Brian Comiskey
Kenneth Crowe
Mark Joseph Darley
John Kavanagh
Jonathon McDonnell
Kealan Murphy
Bart O'Farrell

CASTING
Marie Kelly

CLEANING
Joe McNamara

DESIGN
Laura Howe
Maree Kearns
Eimear Murphy

DEVELOPMENT
Tina Connell
Monica Flynn

DIRECTOR OF THE PEACOCK
Ali Curran

FINANCE
Margaret Bradley
Margaret Flynn
Pat O'Connell

FRONT OF HOUSE
John Baynes
Pauline Morrison

HAIR AND MAKE-UP
Patsy Giles

H.R. MANAGER
Ciaran McCallion

HONORARY ASSOCIATE DIRECTORS
Vincent Dowling
Tomás MacAnna

INFORMATION TECHNOLOGY
Ivan Kavanagh
Dave O'Brien

LIGHTING
Mick Doyle
Brian Fairbrother
Kevin McFadden
Barry Madden

LITERARY
Jocelyn Clarke
Orla Flanagan
Karin McCully

MAINTENANCE
Tony Delaney
Michael Loughnane

OUTREACH/EDUCATION
Sinéad Delaney
Elena Gamble
Irma Grothuis
Michelle Howe
Jean O'Dwyer
Anne O'Gorman

PRESS & MARKETING
Sharon Coady
Lynn Dormer
Liz Halpin
Lucy McKeever

PROPS
Stephen Molloy

RECEPTION
Niamh Douglas
Cheryl Rock
Sandra Williams

SCENIC ARTISTS
Angie Benner
Brian Hegarty
Jennifer Moonan

SOUND
Eddie Breslin
Cormac Carroll
Nuala Golden

STAGE DIRECTORS
Finola Eustace
Audrey Hession
John Stapleton

STAGE DOOR
Patrick Gannon
Patrick Whelan

STAGE HANDS
Aaron Clear
Pat Dillon
Mick Doyle
Des Hegarty
Paul Kelly

STAGE MANAGERS
John Andrews
Gerry Doyle

TECHNICAL
Vanessa Fitz-Simon
Tommy Nolan
Peter Rose
Tony Wakefield

USHERS
Sarah Buckley
Con Doyle
Neil Gallagher
Barry Gleeson
John Holten
Ronan Keenan
Dolores Murphy
Donna Murphy
Jim O'Keefe

VOICE DIRECTOR
Andrea Ainsworth

WARDROBE
Sandra Gibney
Marian Kelly
Niamh Lunny
Vicky Miller
Joan O'Clery
Mandy Scott

ADVISORY COUNCIL
Minister for Arts, Sport and Tourism
Minister for Finance
Kathleen Barrington
Frank Cuneen
Paddy Duffy
Clare Duignan
John Fairleigh
Clive Geraghty
Des Geraghty
Peadar Lamb
Fergus Linehan
John Lynch
Tomás MacAnna
Patricia McBride
Muriel McCarthy
Jimmy Murphy
Donal Nevin
Edna O'Brien
Ulick O'Connor
Pat O'Reilly
Peter Rose
John Stapleton

BEAUTY IN A BROKEN PLACE

SEAN O'CASEY She's dead now, buried with her sister, or so I read. And she won't even know ... [*sighs*] I should have made it up with her and she knew that and I ... I would now, or I think I would, if I had half a chance. Oh, I blame ... You learn when it's too late, maybe you only learn then. Oh, I don't know. She was the greatest woman that Ireland has ever known, if you leave out St Brigid. And maybe St Brigid wasn't as great as they all make out. I mean what did she ever do for me? She was probably an awful nuisance in her day. But Lady Gregory, now. No one could deny that she was ... that she was ... [*stops*] ... great. She was stern and serious and she could be bossy. Very bossy might be a better way of putting it. But she was kind too, and generous and devoted to the cause. She did more for Ireland. She did. She did more for Ireland than that shower that stuck it out in the GPO. And I should have made it up with her before she died. And I shouldn't have been so stubborn. I should have learned. [LADY GREGORY *appears in the shadows*] At least I learned to type, or half did. She'd be glad to know that.

*

LADY GREGORY Mr Casey, your penmanship has been beyond many of us. Some of your best lines were crossed out and some of them were unreadable. So I gave them the benefit of the doubt – they were very good.

O'CASEY I got your letter.

LADY GREGORY So we've had the play typed at our own expense, which is something we don't often do. When Ireland is at peace, perhaps the writers will learn to type.

O'CASEY I'll learn to type when I learn to write.

LADY GREGORY Quite. You have a remarkable sense of character, there are marvellous people in this play, that much is certain, the other directors take the same view, some of your …

O'CASEY [*aside*] I was, she said, to keep away from ideas. She stuck a pin in the word like it was a big red balloon.

LADY GREGORY Ideas, you know, in the right hands … but not in yours. They will be the death of us all. Mr Yeats says that they are not your forte, not your thing. You must let your characters speak, breathe. I suggest that you have a little civil war or a Bolshevik revolution …

O'CASEY [*aside*] A Bolshevik revolution! Can you hear her? St Brigid, fresh from collecting her rents in Coole.

LADY GREGORY And kill off the ideas, leave them bloody in the streets, and allow your characters to triumph, get them nice good jobs in the government.

O'CASEY Do you think it will take much work?

LADY GREGORY If you continue running your hands over the pages like that, it will be in a worse state than it ever was.

O'CASEY I mean, to put it on.

LADY GREGORY I understood that our letter made clear that we did not think –

O'CASEY But you had it typed.

LADY GREGORY You can take it as a way of showing our confidence in you, our hope for you, perhaps even our belief in you.

O'CASEY [*aside*] Ah feck the glory, give me the money.

LADY GREGORY Did you speak?

O'CASEY No, no, I didn't speak. No.

LADY GREGORY Then there is the small problem of Sinn Féin. I don't imagine that they will like the play, and I don't imagine that you like Sinn Féin. You're in favour of the working class, is that correct?

O'CASEY Ah here now, don't be …

LADY GREGORY I would have argued for the play, but these are delicate times and a drama dealing with the fissures between the working class and Sinn Féin might not be helpful. So we must wait.

O'CASEY And victory will be ours.

LADY GREGORY And victory will be ours. You must write another play. Make it all characters and leave the ideas to Mr George Bernard Shaw.

O'CASEY Or Mr Lenin, I suppose.

LADY GREGORY Or Mr Lenin.

*

O'CASEY She believed that a play at her old Abbey could matter that much, could disrupt the peace, or cause even further trouble. I soon learned that once she looked at you in a certain way, she never stopped looking at you, never took her mind off you. She wrote to you and made you write back, and everything you said, every little plan, she remembered. She presumed you were up early in the morning even when you were in the scratcher all day; she presumed you were writing away goodo when you hadn't put pen to paper for weeks. And she presumed that you were like her, full of hope for Ireland when you couldn't care less for the place.

*

LADY GREGORY Mr Casey, come to the window, come now quickly.

O'CASEY [*aside*] God, she loved money. I learned that when she put on *The Shadow of a Gunman*, when she finally told me I had done something worthy of her theatre. She wasn't greedy, mind, or mean even, but the idea of people paying to get into the Abbey made her happy.

LADY GREGORY They have made the decision to stand up from their warm firesides, to leave the public houses to come here. They're paying …

O'CASEY [*aside*] She'd be so happy she couldn't even smile, she'd put a big face on her like she'd swallowed something sour.

LADY GREGORY All of those people are queing to see your play! And in the middle of the disturbances when the streets are dangerous. They are risking everything to see your work and that is all I ever wanted to see, queues in the Abbey, full houses!

*

O'CASEY I miss her voice, the clear, ringing sound of it. I'd love her to know me now. But that, I suppose, wasn't part of the plan, if there ever was a plan – if life, the way we come and go, all isn't random and useless. She asked me that night if I would sit with her. I don't know who she had been keeping the seat for, and if I hadn't been there, she would surely have sold it, for on those nights we turned half the city away.

This night I say I'll sit with her, even though I can't think why she is asking me. It is only when she holds back so that we are going to be caught in the crowd I notice that she walks too slowly to her seat; the strangest thing strikes me and it makes me … it makes me nearly proud … she wants them to see her with me, she wants to be seen beside me, her ladyship of the thousands of acres, as she moved from hotel room to her big house, richer than the Queen or grander anyway, and invited everywhere. It makes me want to run home.

*

LADY GREGORY It has been a great night.

O'CASEY I have to say something to you.

LADY GREGORY You know, Mr Yeats was right. Character, character, that's your forte.

O'CASEY I'd like to say something –

LADY GREGORY And all those full seats –

O'CASEY There's something –

LADY GREGORY I wish we could double up –

O'CASEY You –

LADY GREGORY Maybe another matinée … And I must have a discussion with McCormick about his voice –

O'CASEY Will you listen to me, you old bag!

LADY GREGORY Too loud and too –

O'CASEY Something I wanted to say, something … This place, this building, the Abbey. I mean, you know I have been coming here … when there was nothing else except oul' sermons in the city and the odd speech, you could come in here, it was serious, not a game; it brought me to my senses when there was nothing. Everything I saw here made me … [*sighs*] … made me want to write plays too. It was all your work and Yeats and Synge and Shaw, all of you, what you have done, it's hard to say without sounding … Oh it's a pity you didn't run the Citizen Army too. We might have won.

LADY GREGORY We have done what we could, Mr Casey, to add dignity to Ireland. We wanted to inspire the young men who were tired of politics.

O'CASEY Well, you inspired me anyway, I suppose that's what I was trying to say.

LADY GREGORY I don't think this would be the right time to increase the prices. And McCormick, I shall launch an attack on his voice-box.

*

O'CASEY I don't know why I let Lennox Robinson direct my play. He knew as much about the back streets of Dublin as he did about the Pioneer Total Abstinence Association. Maybe because he knew nothing, he was better than most of them. Sometimes when I watched him directing, it was like someone teaching catechism to a group of little Protestant girls out in the republic of Dalkey.

*

LENNOX ROBINSON I will speak the lines, but they come from offstage and they are loud and you must all stop and listen like you had heard thunder. [*clears throat*]

'The last sixteen months have been the most glorious in the history of Europe. Heroism has come back to the earth. War is a terrible thing, but war is not an evil thing. People in Ireland dread war because they do not know it. Ireland has not known the exhilaration of war for over a hundred years. When war comes to Ireland she must welcome it as she would welcome the Angel of God!'

Now, Miss Delany, even before the Covey speaks, you must be ready. You must speak like someone interrupting.

MISS DELANY Yes, Mr Robinson, I'm ready now. Hold on, sir, till I get myself going now. 'They may crow away out o' them; but it ud be fitther for some o' them to mend their ways, an' cease from havin' scouts out ...'

ROBINSON Miss Delany, could you forget that Rathmines was ever civilized? Perhaps if you went for a walk in these very streets, and listened ...

MISS DELANY You want me to talk like ...? [*pointing at* MISS CROWE]

ROBINSON I do.

MISS DELANY That won't be hard. 'They may crow away out o' them.'

ROBINSON More!

MISS DELANY 'watchin' for th' comin' of th' Saint Vincent de Paul man, for fear they'd be nailed lowerin' a pint of beer, mockin' th' man with an angel face, shinin' with th' glamour of deceit an' lies!'

ROBINSON Now, Miss Crowe, come rushing in, and let us hear you. And I will read the next lines, so Miss Delany, do not stop. Fast now, out with it, loud.

MISS CROWE 'An' a certain lassie standin' stiff behind her own door with her ears cocked listenin' to what's being said, stuffed till she's sthrained with envy of a neighbour thryin' for a few little things that may be got be hard sthrivin' to keep up to th' letther an' th' law, an' th' practices of th' Church!'

ROBINSON [*stiffly*] 'If I was you, Mrs Gogan, I'd parry her jabbin' remarks be a powerful silence that'll keep her tantalizin' words from penethratin' into your feelin's. It's always betther to leave these people to th' vengeance o' God!'

MISS DELANY 'Bessie Burgess doesn't put up to know much, never havin' a swaggerin' mind, thanks be to God ...'

ROBINSON Swaggerin', Miss Delany, swaggerin'.

MISS DELANY That's what I said.

ROBINSON Yes, but it came from the outer reaches of Rathgar. Could you say it, Miss Crowe?

MISS CROWE Swaggerin'.

*

W.B. YEATS One longs, you know, for poetry.

LADY GREGORY This new play, which he wants to call *The Plough and the Stars*, is his best play so far. There is some magnificent drama.

YEATS Yes, he is locked magnificently into the particular.

LADY GREGORY He is our greatest discovery. I think perhaps of all of us he has –

YEATS The common touch.

LADY GREGORY I am sorry you have not read it yet, but when you do you will realize that it will offend not only the few – we are used to that – but the many.

YEATS I have seen enough of it just now to feel that I can manage for a while longer without reading it.

LADY GREGORY It will offend our friends as well as our enemies.

YEATS That is why we have friends.

LADY GREGORY So what shall we do?

YEATS Defend our poor playwright, what else can we do?

LADY GREGORY This will be the hardest battle. They will hate it, all of them. Those who do not come will hate it when they hear of it, but if they come I'm afraid they will hate it even more. And then there is the small matter of the new member of the board, Mr O'Brien.

YEATS Yes, O'Brien is not stupid and there is nothing that causes greater mischief than a half-clever man. One wishes the river Liffey would be set aside to keep the two types apart.

LADY GREGORY I rather thought that it entirely devoted itself to that purpose.

YEATS Yes, but not enough, not enough at all. I must speak to the government about widening it. He is one of the new mob, O'Brien, he has been let into the Kildare Street Club as a gesture to the Free State. He is most effective when he puts his thoughts on paper. We should ensure that he does not get the opportunity.

*

MISS DELANY '... but goin' on packin' up knowledge accordin' to her conscience: precept upon precept, line upon line; here a little, an' there a little. But [*with a passionate swing of her shawl*], thanks be to Christ, she knows when she was got, where she was got, an' how she was got; while there's some she knows, decoratin' their finger with a well-polished weddin' ring, would be hard put to it if they were assed to show their weddin' lines!'

ROBINSON Now, have a very great fit, Miss Crowe.

MISS CROWE Oh God, this is terrible stuff.

ROBINSON Could you do it first and then we shall all worry about it together afterwards? Just say the lines, my dear.

MISS CROWE [*plunging out into the centre of the floor in a wild tempest of hysterical rage*] 'Y' oul' rip of a blasted liar, me weddin' ring's been well earned be twenty years be th' side o' me husband, now takin' his rest in heaven ...'

*

YEATS We will have to make cuts.

LADY GREGORY Let O'Brien suggest them. He is, after all, the new member of the board with the ear of the government and it will make him feel wanted and trusted. He will think we are giving in to him.

YEATS He will suggest the wrong cuts. Perhaps it would be better for all of us if we offered him five pounds for his horse.

LADY GREGORY Let us wait and see.

*

O'CASEY Together they could have run the Empire and the Irish Transport and General Workers' Union all at the same time. When I gave them the new play, they said nothing – they knew as well as I did that it was the tenth anniversary of the Rising and they knew too that this measly oul' subsidy from the government, if government was the word for them, meant that they were running a little branch of the civil service in the middle of a theatre and if they wanted the great art beaten down, there was no one like a civil servant to do that for them.

And that George O'Brien, the new director, he was worse than a civil servant, he was an economist. An economist. He wouldn't know a play if it bit him around the annual budget deficit.

*

MRS YEATS Oh, do come in!

O'CASEY [*aside*] And I suppose as a gesture of goodwill, St Brigid told me it was my duty to come to one of Yeats' Monday evenings. I was greeted at the door by his lovely English wife.

MRS YEATS How kind of you to come! How much we have all been looking forward to having you! You must give me your coat. It is a privilege to have you here. I suppose people feel they know you from the plays, but I don't feel that. I am sure you are somebody else.

O'CASEY [*aside, not giving her the coat*] The latest and rarest specimen they had collected, Johnny Cassidy with his hobnailed breath and his tenement squint.

MRS YEATS I mean you have a very great wit, and sympathy, but I feel you have much more. Oh, do give me your coat!

O'CASEY [*aside*] You'd think she'd have a maid to take your coat, but she took it herself as though it had once belonged to Finn McCool. She was a sweet woman, Mrs Yeats, English through and through. You could always trust the English and they never meant any harm, God help them. And all they've had to put up with through the centuries. Imagine having Robinson and Russell and all that shower running the country for you and trying to talk like you.

MRS YEATS Mr Robinson is here. Of course you must be old friends, but do come and meet him. Mr O'Casey!

O'CASEY [*aside*] Funny, I studied the other people there all that night and I thought I knew everything about them. Oh, I wasn't nervous at all. They often looked at me, took me in when I wasn't meant to be paying attention, so they could find out how it was done, how you could have crowds queing for all your plays. Nobody went near their plays, and rightly so. Who would? Russell told me he wanted a curtain of gauze between the audience and the stage. I'd put a curtain of gauze around his arse. Sure he'd no arse either. Funny, they all had no arse. Robinson –

MRS YEATS Mr Robinson is so impressed by your new play. He was just saying –

ROBINSON [*aside*] That you must have had help from someone in the Irish Transport and General Workers' Union to write them, but maybe if you give anyone from the slums a pen and paper and teach them to read and write, it will pour out of them.

O'CASEY [*aside*] I learned something I didn't know that night. By that time I thought I knew everything. But what I didn't know was how to stand in a room talking and doing nothing else, or pretending to listen.

MRS YEATS Now, do have a drink.

O'CASEY I'll have a glass of water.

MRS YEATS Surely you would like some sherry, or something stronger. We have some rather good Madeira. I'll show it to you.

O'CASEY Oh, a cup of tea then.

ROBINSON [*taking the bottle from* MRS YEATS] Is it cold outside, Casey? You know, I long for the south in the winter.

MRS YEATS [*taking the bottle back*] Would you like to try some?

O'CASEY A drop of alcohol –

ROBINSON [*taking the bottle and pouring some into his glass*] Has never passed his lips, I suppose he is going to say.

O'CASEY Has never passed my lips.

YEATS Casey, do have a drink. No, you must.

MRS YEATS No, he doesn't drink. We are making him tea in the kitchen. He has no vices. [*staring at* ROBINSON]

O'CASEY [*aside*] Yeats always called me Casey, like I was delivering coal to his basement, and Robinson joined in whenever he could, and St Brigid herself often 'Caseyed' me, as though I worked for her, cleaned the grounds of Coole. It was only Mrs Yeats who was a real lady and called me by my proper name. I loved how she said it, her lovely English tongue rolling around her mouth with it –

MRS YEATS Mr O'Casey.

O'CASEY You could always trust the English. They had respect and decency and manners.

YEATS Italy, I believe, has become a model society. I have written to the government about it. It is something we should study and emulate.

ROBINSON There is a fine wine from there I have a passion for … doesn't travel of course, but nonetheless my wine merchant …

O'CASEY [*aside*] I knew how to walk, and I knew how to sit down. I could lie down with the best of them. Lord knows I loved a good day in bed! And I could stand around waiting for something or staring at something. But how do you stand up in a room? You put one foot here and you leave the other alone and you have a glass in one hand ...

MRS YEATS Mr O'Casey, do have more tea.

YEATS The new state must be a home for the beautiful as much as for the brave. And there must be colour and even grandeur in how we make our laws.

O'CASEY [*aside*] And I suppose you can put the other in your pocket, but not too deep in, as though you were rooting for something. Just enough. And keep your mouth shut unless you are talking, or in the case of Robinson even if you are. And the difference between me and them was they knew how to stand in the room as though they owned it and I didn't.

ROBINSON When I travel in the length and breadth of our land, it is beauty I crave and I find, and it makes me shudder, Father Pat CC and Father Mick PP are whispering against life itself. I find that the hurley stick has replaced the sceptre in men's minds.

O'CASEY [*aside*] When I visit the water-closet, I notice that they have heating on in the hall. Can you imagine the waste? What would you need heating for in a hall? To keep the paintings warm, or the tiles on the floor? Or the rug and the steps of the stairs? And then in the closet itself, don't they have sheets of toilet paper? God! Imagine spending money on toilet paper! The sheer waste of it! It turns my stomach to think of the waste of it! If me mother was alive, she'd talk about this for days. She hated waste, and she knew, and I knew too, not to waste good paper. And at least when I had good paper I knew what to do with it.

*

MISS RICHARDS [*flaming up*] 'I burned it, I burned it! That's what I did with it! Is General Connolly an' th' Citizen Army goin' to be your only care? Is your home goin' to be only a place to rest in? Am I goin' to be only somethin' to provide merry-makin' at night for you? Your vanity'll be th' ruin of you an' me yet ... That's what's movin' you: because they've made an officer of you, you'll make a glorious cause of what you're doin', while your little red-lipp'd Nora can go on sittin' here, makin' a companion of th' loneliness of th' night!'

*

MISS CROWE [*running*] They're after seeing my lines, the whole lot of them, they took them off me. I was taking them home to learn them and they stopped me and they won't give them back. And they say it's all immoral, as though I didn't know that already.

LADY GREGORY Now could someone get young Miss Crowe a

cup of water and then crush her gently until she ceases to speak.

MISS CROWE Oh God, they know all about it now and they're going to get de Valera after us, or worse, the Archbishop, or worse than him again. There is worse, you know.

LADY GREGORY Use force if you have to. Send down to props. Hit her with a loy.

MISS CROWE And herself, herself is going to see it tonight and they're going to have a meeting.

LADY GREGORY Miss Crowe, if you do not calm down, I shall order a large bucket of very cold water to be thrown over you.

MISS CROWE Herself already knows about it, and she's going to put a curse on us! She has the evil eye!

ROBINSON And who's herself when she is at home?

MISS CROWE Mrs Hanna Sheehy Skeffington has the play and there's going to be a meeting tonight up in her house and they're all going to be there and they're going to get a Monsignor to read the bits, oh the bits, the terrible bits, and Mrs Tom Clarke and Mrs Pearse and oul' Maud Gonne, the whole proclamation of them, are going to denounce us.

O'CASEY Irishmen and Irishwomen who wanted only to post a letter in the GPO to their cousins in England, in the name of the dead generations …

MISS CROWE They're going to denounce us! Denounce us! We haven't a hope. And they're going to take the subsidy off of us! Wait until the others hear about it!

LADY GREGORY Miss Crowe, if you speak once more in this

building a single line which is not in the script, then I shall personally wring your neck.

O'CASEY ... we the mad widows and the embittered oul' mothers call on the priests and the crawthumpers and the twisted bigots who inhabit this land ...

LADY GREGORY Mr Casey!

O'CASEY ... to gather together their rosaries and their scapulars and their foul superstitions ...

LADY GREGORY Mr Casey, one more word!

O'CASEY And strike a blow for Ireland by buying tickets for *The Plough and the Stars*.

MISS CROWE I know what it's called, thanks.

*

O'CASEY F.J. McCormick, made bitter by his own small portion of talent, in love with himself and his booming voice, now gone all hoarse, and going out with Eileen Crowe, who wouldn't play the part of Mrs Gogan on the advice, if you don't mind, of her confessor. I had to make up another part for her and let May Craig do Jinnie Gogan.

*

F.J. MCCORMICK Do you know something, Eileen? I hate that O'Casey. I hate the whole look of him.

MISS CROWE F.J., we'll have to put up with him for the duration and say his lines. He wrote the new part for me anyway, the Lady from Rathmines, so I don't have to be that Mrs Gogan anymore.

MCCORMICK God, Eileen, there are some terrible lines in the play, lines that I'm convinced were written on purpose to annoy me. If that Richards says 'snotty' again to me in that Ballsbridge voice of hers, I'll have to …

MISS CROWE Oh now …

MCCORMICK But do you know what's really killing me?

MISS CROWE What?

MCCORMICK You would have made the best Nora, you would have made her a great woman, and they all would have loved you, and we could have played the parts night after night. God, I'd love to say some of those lines to you.

MISS CROWE I thought you said you hated them.

MCCORMICK 'Little red-lipped Nora.' I love that line, and I think about my Eileen when I say it. 'I didn't forget this was your birthday, did I? And you liked your new hat; didn't you, didn't you?'

MISS CROWE I have her lines off by heart, you know.

MCCORMICK Say them! Say them!

MISS CROWE 'Jack, Jack; please, Jack! I thought you were tired of that sort of thing long ago.'

MCCORMICK [*moving towards her*] 'Well, you're finding out now that I amn't tired of it yet, anyhow. Mrs Clitheroe doesn't want to be kissed, sure she doesn't? [*He kisses her.*] Little, little red-lipped Nora!' They should be put in jail for not giving you the part. Imagine we could play this night after night. [*He kisses her again.*]

MISS CROWE I'd love that all right.

⋆

LADY GREGORY Mr O'Brien, it is so good of you to come at such short notice, and we are so grateful to you for all your time. You must be so busy.

GEORGE O'BRIEN Yes, yes. There are many rumours circulating about the new O'Casey play, *The Plough and the Stripes*.

YEATS One of the actresses has been to see her confessor about the matter, but that, as far as I understand the sacrament of confession, can hardly be called a rumour circulating.

O'BRIEN Yes, yes. This is the tenth anniversary of the Rebellion and it behoves the National Theatre to mount a production which might be edifying to say the least and honour those who died so that the younger generations might learn to live with their example.

YEATS Their example includes freedom, does it not? They were poets, after all, and thinkers.

O'BRIEN Their names are spoken of with awe by the people.

O'CASEY [*aside*] Awe yes, awe no, keep O'Brien out of the GPO.

LADY GREGORY Mr O'Brien, as you know, there is no mention of any of their names in O'Casey's new play. And great drama, as you know, produces its own awe.

O'BRIEN Yes, yes. As a member of the board, however, I remain concerned, and I should like as soon as possible to see the text of the play. As you know, this is not an easy time for the government and perhaps I should add that I have not sought this meeting on a whim, that others –

YEATS Perhaps you will let them know that if they wish to commemorate the Rising, then I read almost daily in that rag, what is it called …?

LADY GREGORY The *Irish Independent*.

YEATS Oh yes, quite right, that is what it is called – the *Irish Independent* – that O'Connell Street is the widest street in Europe and is made for such events. We are a small theatre, our light is the light of the spirit.

LADY GREGORY Quite.

O'BRIEN When can I see the script with the cuts?

YEATS As soon as I can arrange it, Mr O'Brien. I can have it sent to you at the National University.

O'BRIEN When will that be?

YEATS I shall speak to Mr Robinson so that all the directors shall have their copy of the new text.

O'CASEY [*aside*] An economist was reading the play and preparing himself to sabotage it out of sheer badness. And the widows in the deep suburbs, places would give you the creeps, led by Mrs Sheehy Skeffington, thinking they knew about plays.

*

MRS SHEEHY SKEFFINGTON Mr O'Brien, thank you for coming here. I am grateful to you. Now, I will not waste your time. I simply appeal to you. You are the voice of reason.

O'BRIEN Yes, yes. Mrs Sheehy Skeffington, I am a member of the board of the theatre. I have the right to be consulted and the right to warn. Perhaps I could tell you in confidence …

MRS SHEEHY SKEFFINGTON Yes?

O'BRIEN I hope it would not be a great disloyalty …

MRS SHEEHY SKEFFINGTON Yes?

O'BRIEN The board meetings are excruciating. That Lennox Robinson!

MRS SHEEHY SKEFFINGTON The Abbey Theatre is a very great institution, Mr O'Brien. What other ones do we have? It is essential that you –

O'BRIEN I know, sit there and suffer.

MRS SHEEHY SKEFFINGTON You also have the right to resign, but before that, may I say that you have a duty to prevail. Now I have no interest in whether the language of this play is good or bad. He can put in as many foul words as he likes, Mr O'Brien. Nor is it personal, I would like you to know. It is a matter of public importance.

O'BRIEN Mrs Sheehy Skeffington, it's only a play …

O'CASEY [*aside*] The crawthumpin' economist …

MRS SHEEHY SKEFFINGTON Mr O'Brien, we are talking about the greatest institution this country has built without any help from the British. We are talking about the Abbey Theatre. Nothing matters as much. How can you …?

O'BRIEN Yes, yes. There is so much work to be done in the country. These are just plays.

MRS SHEEHY SKEFFINGTON My husband and I made a point of going to every play since the theatre started. It was part of the great Ireland we hoped for, watching ordinary men and women transform themselves. That play Yeats wrote, *Cathleen Ni Houlihan*, we were there and we saw, almost in front of our eyes, the young men carried into a dream by it. They were not just plays, as you would have it. So many of us were so used to the music hall and now this raw … something I had never imagined possible.

O'BRIEN But it couldn't have …

MRS SHEEHY SKEFFINGTON It affected the young men when Maud Gonne was transformed on the stage. It did not affect us, of course. We were spellbound by the acting, but for myself and my husband, the politics were too emotional, too ill-considered, but for others it made all the difference.

O'BRIEN Yes, yes. But that's history now, that's all over. We are living in a new state.

MRS SHEEHY SKEFFINGTON As I was saying, the play led them to join the movement, it led them to their death. And now the theatre wants to mock them, sully their memory.

O'BRIEN Surely their memory is in what they achieved.

MRS SHEEHY SKEFFINGTON This play will cheapen even the slightest achievement. It will darken our most sleepless nights to know that the dead are being mocked. I have ceased to visit my husband's grave, although soon it will be the tenth anniversary of his murder and it is as though … Look around! All the books we shared, the hopes we had. My husband was the most intelligent man I have ever met and the most idealistic. When I read a book, Mr O'Brien, even still I forget myself that he is not alive, that I cannot mark a passage for him to read when he returns. We joined our names and we joined our hopes for this country. I simply do not believe that he is dead. He was a man of peace. He went out that day … oh, you know why he went out. He was brave, not like the others were brave, the men who started the rebellion, my husband was a pacifist and he was a socialist and he believed that the looting by the people of Dublin would be shocking and disgraceful to the world. He cared about that. And this play now idealizes the looters, makes them the heroes. There is no nobility in that play and I knew some of the other men who died and I knew … oh I know him still … Francis … and I still wish I could walk out now and find him, even be with him … and I am faced with O'Casey's cheapness, cheap jibes, a play which belongs to the back lanes, to the slums, full of cheap characters. And in the official theatre, the state theatre, a play which idealizes the looters, makes them the heroes.

O'BRIEN Yes, yes.

*

[MISS DELANY *and* MISS CRAIG *enter, pushing a pram full of loot.*]

MISS CRAIG 'I don't remember ever havin' seen such lovely pairs as them …'

ROBINSON No, Miss Craig, you must speak these lines off-stage and loud, so that we hear you before we see you. So could you go back for one moment?

MISS CRAIG And say them again?

ROBINSON If you would … and be aware that when you

appear you will, I imagine, cause much laughter in the audience, so stop for a moment.

MISS CRAIG When?

ROBINSON [*tries a Dublin accent*] 'such lovely pairs as them' and then pick up the shoes and show them to Miss Delany, and then go on when the laughter has subsided. And push the pram with pride, if you would, like someone showing off.

MISS CRAIG Let me do it now without interrupting me. Are you ready?

ROBINSON We are all waiting, Miss Craig.

MISS CRAIG [*outside*] 'I don't remember ever havin' seen such lovely pairs as them, [*they appear*] with th' pointed toes an' th' cuban heels.'

MISS DELANY 'They'll go grand with th' dhresses we're afther liftin', when we've stitched a sthray bit o' silk to lift th' bodices up a little bit higher, so as to shake th' shame out o' them, an' make them fit for women that hasn't lost themselves in th' nakedness o' th' times.'

ROBINSON Oh, that's wonderful, wonderful.

*

O'CASEY I remember that time Lady Gregory invited me to Coole. She loved the place and she thought the fresh air – God, I liked fresh air, but you could have too much of it – would do me good. All the dripping trees and the lake and the nine bean rows and the swans. Swans! I never liked swans. Would give you the creeps. Anyway, I packed my stuff and took one train and then another. God, out of the window of those trains was a pure wilderness, and I wondered if anyone on the train had known that I was going as a guest of the great Lady Gregory at her mansion in Coole to be waited on hand and foot and have the run of the place with the trees dripping freely on me. And nine and fifty swans! Did you ever hear worse? 'Oh upon the brimming water among the stones / are nine and fifty swans.' You were lucky if you saw three or four. Maybe it was the hens Yeats was referring to. There were a lot of hens all right. All pecking away goodo. Useful creatures, hens! If the people on the train had known where I was going, they would have asked the question I asked myself as soon as I arrived: where was my collar?

*

MARION Oh look at the cut of his drawers! Sure what sort of gentleman is he? You can tell her ladyship that I'll not serve him. He can serve himself. Sure Sacred Heart of Jesus, where he is from they're reared on leftovers. And you should see him pointing at things with her ladyship like he is going to buy a share in the place. The names of all the trees if you don't mind. And God on high he has taken two of the books to his room, the books no one is allowed to touch, and soon they'll be in his case. And the dirt of him. The dirty drawers he brought. It would give you dropsy to think of the ones he might be wearing. Or maybe he's not wearing any. Oh no! Oh don't start me thinking about that! I'll get the shivers.

O'CASEY [*aside*] Where was my bow-tie? What was I going to wear when I was eating dinner or supper or whatever it is the posh people called it, they had words for everything – dinner, my dinner. What was I going to wear for my dinner? I'd a few spare shirts and a fresh pair of socks and I'd even packed a pair of woolly drawers. Those houses I heard can be fierce damp and bad for the bones. If you were caught short in the middle of the night, you'd be better to be wearing something. But I'd never worn a tie in my life. I mean I wasn't standing for the Dáil. I wasn't a complete hypocrite. I was just going to stay with her ladyship.

MARION Is the gentleman here to mend something?

LADY GREGORY No, Mr O'Casey, Mr Sean O'Casey, is staying here. As you well know. Is that all?

ANNE Marion is having a fit! [*silence*] A fit, your ladyship! A fit! A fit!

LADY GREGORY Marion can do as she pleases during her leisure time.

ANNE The gentleman came with no collar. We've looked in his suitcase. He's not a gentleman at all.

LADY GREGORY He is a guest.

ANNE And he'll be eating in the scullery, your ladyship, we've made a little table for him.

LADY GREGORY He'll eat in the dining-room and do so promptly, I hope, and with hot soup and less runny gravy and less lumpy mashed potatoes than have become normal in this house.

O'CASEY [*aside*] If I'd thought of it, I would have bought a dozen collars and saved the fuss, and the gintleman is no gintleman. And then I catch her coming out of my room.

MARION I hope you're enjoying your stay now and the weather holds up.

O'CASEY [*aside*] And the bitter old smile on her! But I know by the look of her that she has done something terrible, as indeed she has. She has unpacked my case, like I was Lord Muck. Oh Lord, she must have looked at my drawers! Oh the socks! Oh the vests! She'll tell the whole house about the state of me.

MARION Mr Sean O'Dirtydrawers wants a maid, that's what he wants, but he can get his own maid, I'm not waiting on him. Sacred Heart, the years of dirt must be ingrained in the thing! Oh God, thinking about it! And his old wall eyes. There's a real Dublin look about him, he's a dirty malingering sort of chancer, that's what he is, and he needs soap and water and a good long spell in the army, oh God if we only had an army would take him!

*

LADY GREGORY Marion and Anne, stand up straight, both of you, and pay full attention. Mr O'Casey is a guest in this house and he will not be discussed or disturbed and if you do not wish to see him without his collar, then you do not have to, he will sit with his back to the door, and if you wish to be bad mannered, and I can see that you do, then you do not have to look at him, you can come up behind him to serve him and take his plates away and fill his glass and you will never know what he is wearing. And that will be all, except for one thing: Marion, did the Lord send you to try me? Is that why you are here?

MARION No, your ladyship.

LADY GREGORY Good, well, that at least is good news.

*

O'CASEY [*aside*] And so we sit at the long table, her ladyship and myself, and we discuss high art over all the courses and how the working man can be elevated and how the one true book is the one true book, and every time that cross-eyed one passes me I squint up at her, making clear that the Bolshevik revolution and all its works have arrived in Coole in my person. And if she has looked closely, she will have seen that her ladyship, the essence of tact and hospitality, has provided my neck with a great silk scarf, in case I is cold, or in a draft, she says, to hide my nakedness. [*stops*]

One of the days I was there I saw a beech tree cut down at Coole. For her, it is like her own arm is being cut off. I mean it is just a tree. A tree. There are plenty of others, too many if you ask me, and not enough in some places where they might be of benefit. But that wasn't what she felt. It has gone rotten, so she says, and there is nothing else could be done. It is a black morning for her when they all arrive to do the chopping and felling and she knows all the men's names and where they are from and she makes sure they're all fed before they start which is, I think, foolish of her, but you don't idle under her great gaze. I suppose her being popular in the locality saved the house when all the others were burned. She knows what she's doing, you can always say that about her. I stand back and watch her as she gives instructions, and she moves up and down like it is a cavalry charge. She doesn't take her eyes off them once, or the tree, and she is always far enough back so that no one can let a roar at her that a branch is coming down on top of her. As I watch them with the ropes and the saws, I think she might cry, but I realize as I come and go all that morning that she has used up all her tears, like a lot of women of her age whose only son was dead in the war. Or maybe she never did have tears and all her sorrow has become her strength.

*

MISS DELANY Your ladyship, I love my lines, I thought they were great when I read them, but I know now that I can't say the lines and I'm after telling Mr Robinson. Something terrible would happen. I'd have an accident if I said them, and I'm after telling the priest about them and he said I was to go straight to you, that you're a good Christian woman, despite everything, despite ... I mean that you're a practising member of the, the ... Church of Ireland, but Casey is an anti-Christ, ma'am, he's a Bolshevik, he's a communist, you can tell by looking at him, and he wrote articles, I never liked him, and he educated himself, which is a very bad sign. Father McLoughlin says that I don't have to say the lines.

LADY GREGORY Have you been speaking to Miss Eileen Crowe? Do you wish to move to a minor part ... Would you like to play Mollser? Or do you wish to return to your former employment? What was it that you did?

MISS DELANY It's my conscience, your ladyship. That's what the priest says.

LADY GREGORY Miss Delany, would I, would anyone, stand between you and your conscience?

MISS DELANY I'll leave the bits out so. Is that all right? I'll say all the rest.

LADY GREGORY I will discuss the matter with Mr Casey, but carry on now please, pretend you forgot the lines for the moment, but say nothing to anyone.

*

O'CASEY This now is the Free State they all fought for, and if I am not free to put my lines on the stage without some crawthumping actress telling me what I can and can't do, then what sort of state is it?

*

MRS SHEEHY SKEFFINGTON [*reading*] 'You louse, you louse, you! ... You're no man ... You're no man ... I'm a woman, anyhow, an' if I'm a prostitute aself, I have me feelin's ...' Oh Lord! This will make the Free State proud of itself. Disgusting! In a pub with the flag! Madame MacBride, we shall stop the play! We shall stand in front of it with a dignity and a determination more proud and fierce than anything they have imagined on the stage. I will walk through the city to that theatre. I will not rest now. They may believe that they have all the power, but I have the light of justice and the force of will. The dead will not be mocked by a second-rate play.

MAUD GONNE MacBRIDE It is most offensive. It is an offence to decency and to the memory of the dead. We shall gather the group as we did for Poppy Day. Down with the Poppy Theatre! Down with it! They will have to drag us off the stage. If they want louse, I'll show them louse.

MRS SHEEHY SKEFFINGTON Louse indeed!

*

O'CASEY Maybe I should have put the play on in England. I loved England as soon as I heard of it even. It was a place with a real history. They loved Ireland, most of them, and they missed owning and running it, and they were delighted to see an Irish person. It didn't matter who you were. But God if you were a playwright they'd jump at you. I suppose they had no playwrights of their own. Too busy. Too happy. And too many of them dead in the war. They had none of the terrible meanness of the Irish. And none of the wit either. And you'd miss that sometimes. And maybe they had the same sanctimoniousness and hypocrisy as the Irish, but they kept it to themselves. God, I remember I got sick when I heard Labour men saying there were no streetwalkers in Dublin until the Tommies came. Holier than Moses, the followers of Connolly, and cash on the nail. God I was sick of them. That boat to Liverpool was the best invention since the shamrock. Oh I gave them a streetwalker all right. By God, if they'd never seen one, they were going to see one now.

*

MISS MOONEY 'Curse o' God on th' haporth, hardly, Tom. There isn't much notice taken of a pretty petticoat of a night like this ... They're all in a holy mood. Th' solemn-lookin' dials on th' whole o' them an' they marchin' to th' meetin'. You'd think they were th' glorious company of th' saints –'

Mr Robinson, they'll go mad when they hear this, won't they? It'll be a great night! Do you think there'll be a riot? I'd love a riot.

ROBINSON My dear, it will be even better because you are doing it with such gusto, as though it came naturally – in a manner of speaking, of course.

MISS MOONEY [*showing her leg*] Oh, you'd want to be careful what you're saying to Rosie Redmond.

*

LADY GREGORY There is trouble and there is going to be more. Miss Mooney likes her part rather too much, while the others say that there are no girls like Rosie Redmond in the parts of Dublin where they were brought up. Miss Crowe has refused to play the wholesome Mrs Gogan, and Miss Craig, who now has the part, is insisting that she will make no reference to the Ten Commandments. The line in question seems to be: [*archly*] 'an' any kid, livin' or dead, that Jinnie Gogan's had since, was got between th' bordhers of th' Ten Commandments!' We may have her replaced too, although I suspect she will soften with persuasion. And then McCormick, the ghastly McCormick ...

YEATS What does he have to say?

LADY GREGORY He refuses to say the word 'snotty'.

YEATS Snotty? In relation to the Ten Commandments?

LADY GREGORY No, no, he refuses to say the word at all and Miss Richards is not helping by enunciating the word with all her power when it comes to her turn to say it. 'Snotty', she shouts the word out. She has no objection to saying it. And, you know, I don't think it has any special meaning for RCs. We can't let the actors pick words and set up a sort of vigilance committee. But some words must go, I do realize that – the song must go, it is quite filthy.

YEATS I must confess it was the song, the filthy song, which kept me from falling asleep as I read all the dreary dialogue. Let me see. Here it is:

'I once had a lover, a tailor, but he could do nothin' for me,
An' then I fell in with a sailor as strong an' as wild as th' sea.
We cuddled an' kissed with devotion, till th' night from th' mornin' had fled;
An' there, to our joy, a bright bouncin' boy
Was dancin' a jig in th' bed!'

Oh yes, this is rather the best bit. The chorus.

'Dancin' a jig in th' bed, an' bawlin' for butther an' bread.
An' there, to our joy, a bright bouncin' boy
Was dancin' a jig in th' bed!'

I wonder if I should like him more if he wrote ballads rather than these plays about the poor and their vices, the tenements warbling and too much shouting. It made me sleepy, all the noise.

LADY GREGORY Well, wake up, there is going to be a row.

YEATS With the actors?

LADY GREGORY No, I shall squash all revolt among the employees of the theatre.

YEATS You mean O'Brien from the Catholic University?

LADY GREGORY No, I shall squash him too.

YEATS Well, then who?

LADY GREGORY This time I think the whole country may turn against us.

YEATS Oh, why didn't you say so to begin with? The whole country? I will have no difficulty with that. I was concerned that we might be dealing with a more formidable foe.

LADY GREGORY Which would be?

YEATS Dullness. Greyness. Dullness. The enemy that is always at the gates, rattling them.

LADY GREGORY We must remain calm and steadfast. We all need you now.

YEATS Yes, I am ready. The play will be heard above the common noise.

*

O'CASEY You go backstage sometimes and they're all hungry like dogs for praise and you have to be careful not to say too much to one in case the other hears. I loved them, I suppose, but the way you love begging children you see on the street just after you've given them something. I never trusted them though. I saw how easily they could change, and most of them had not an ounce of intelligence, which made them even better actors, or so I heard. I loved the brightness in them, that's what I loved, the eagerness, and they gave me a home for a while. But I knew there were rules and I knew that some time or other we'd fight over the rules. And the rules were they had to be praised all the time.

And of all the actors, I hated McCormick. I even hated his name – McCormick – it's a terrible name. There was never anyone decent called McCormick. Overacting, underacting and acting the eejit, all under the auspices of F.J. McCormick. And they came into the Abbey with *Man and Superman* and afterwards I told them.

*

MCCORMICK Did you enjoy it? Did you?

O'CASEY You must be joking. Would you go away?

MISS CROWE Oh I think they all loved us tonight. And you were great. They loved the bit where –

O'CASEY You were all atrocious. All of you!

MISS DELANY He's drunk.

MCCORMICK Get him out of here.

MISS CROWE Go home with you now. We're just finished working and we don't need your views now.

MCCORMICK Sure he knows nothing. He's a complete ignoramus. Go on with you!

O'CASEY Do you know what you were like, McCormick?

MISS CROWE Don't listen to him.

MISS DELANY Pay no attention to him.

O'CASEY Are you afraid to hear, are you? Do you know what you were like? You were like a headless chicken prancing around with a toothache. You're only in the part because you're half-paid. The fellow in England is getting double what you get.

BARLOW What are you doing on the stage?

O'CASEY I'm on my way to the Green Room. What do you think I'm doing?

BARLOW There's none but the actors and officials allowed on the stage and we'd be glad if you came this way no more.

O'CASEY [*aside*] So I didn't suppose they were too happy with me when they got my blasphemous play; it didn't stop them taking parts in it but it didn't stop them complaining either once they had the parts. And McCormick, the sly oul' McCormick, went off to find O'Brien and see what trouble he could cause. The language was beyond the beyonds, he said.

*

O'BRIEN [*with a limp*] Lady Gregory, I am extremely concerned. The language is beyond the beyonds.

LADY GREGORY I know, I have your letter which Mr Yeats has given me. Now it seems you don't like some of the words.

O'BRIEN Yes, yes. I presumed these words had already been cut. These are words that cannot be spoken in any theatre which wishes to commemorate a recent event in our history.

LADY GREGORY [*reading*] Let me see … yes 'Jesus', 'Jasus', 'Christ', 'bitch', 'lowsers' and 'lice'. Lice? Yes, I suppose it is not a pleasant word. No, these are not polite words.

O'BRIEN Lady Gregory, the professional side of the lady in Act II is unduly emphasized.

LADY GREGORY As you said in your letter. I can read, Mr O'Brien.

O'BRIEN If it were a play about prostitutes, then she would be needed on the stage, but this is a play about the Easter Rebellion.

LADY GREGORY It is a play about the living city, the common people in a time of strife.

O'BRIEN Yes, yes. Lady Gregory, I do not wish to waste your time, but I am concerned, as a director of the theatre, about the possibility that the play might offend a section of public opinion with which we have to contend at budget time. The unfurling of the flag in a public house, the drama of cowards and looters, the blasphemous language, may provoke an attack on the theatre of a kind that would endanger the continuance of the subsidy.

LADY GREGORY Mr O'Brien, I speak as a defender of John Millington Synge and of George Bernard Shaw in this theatre, and I speak as the translator of *Cuchulain* and I speak as someone who stood up for freedom in Ireland in a dark time. Mr O'Brien, can I make it clear to you that if it is a choice we have to make between our freedom and the subsidy, then we will always take our freedom. Always. Always. We will never hesitate.

O'BRIEN Yes, yes. So be it, then.

LADY GREGORY However, we will make changes in the love scene as you suggest, and perhaps the song. Perhaps you are right about the song.

*

O'CASEY My eyes were troubling me then, but they troubled me a bit less when we got rid of that one who wouldn't say her lines and we put in May Craig who would do what she was told and watching Shelah Richards some days made me forget everything, all the rows and bitterness, made me … You could sit looking at her forever when she was on the stage or rehearsing. I'd love passing close to her, pretending it was for nothing, and I'd love the smell from her – God, so clean, so … But then just when I'd be distracted by thoughts of beauty it would all start again, you'd think Queen Victoria was coming to the opening or the Pope or Matt Talbot was going to be in the audience, and they wanted the song out and this word out and the other word so I told them they could go to hell. There were others would put on the play in full if they wouldn't. So I withdrew it.

*

LADY GREGORY Mr O'Casey, your withdrawing the play is not helpful. Now you must withdraw your withdrawal, like a very good man –

O'CASEY McCormick is an ecclesiastical cuckoo-clock, a failed bully, a –

LADY GREGORY If you are worried about McCormick, I can crush him quickly and effectively.

O'CASEY I'm not making any more cuts, and O'Brien –

LADY GREGORY Mr Casey, this is not about McCormick or O'Brien. It is the first battle in the new state over our freedom. I wish us to win the battle. I need you to fight on our side. Could you hand me back the play?

O'CASEY How are you going to fight them? With more cuts?

LADY GREGORY No more cuts. We shall use the two best weapons at our disposal.

O'CASEY The power and the glory, I suppose.

LADY GREGORY Indeed. Coming in the guise of our determination first, which will vanquish all who stand in our way, and then –

O'CASEY A bit of brute force.

LADY GREGORY That might not be necessary. I shall retreat to

Coole and we shall use all the might at our disposal, we shall call in –

O'CASEY The Free State Army? Are you serious?

LADY GREGORY We shall wheel out Yeats.

O'CASEY Upon the brimming waters among the stones are nine and fifty swans. That'll shut them up all right. A terrible beauty is Borneo, that'll be the words will cause them to turn on their heels and run for their life. That'd frighten the Black and Tans … Oh arise and go now.

LADY GREGORY Mr O'Casey, when Mr Yeats is fired up he is a most formidable figure, and between us we have the matches and the kindling to do the firing.

O'CASEY Will you deal with McCormick then?

*

MAUD GONNE MacBRIDE [*whistling*] I scoured Henry Street and then ventured into Mary Street where I discovered a trader in possession of this most perfect object. Oh, listen to it. This will make thunder.

MRS SHEEHY SKEFFINGTON It is important that we move with dignity, that we stand apart from any crowd. People will judge us well if we summon their nobility rather than their rage. We must summon our own nobility.

MAUD GONNE MacBRIDE The meeting of all the widows will go very well, don't you think? It will be the proudest day for Ireland to see them all come, the lovely sad Mrs Pearse and her gentle daughter, and Mrs Tom Clarke, who is ready for the fray, and Mrs Barry, oh so sad, so sad, and the Plunkett women and the Gifford women are ready to do their duty. All of them are ready. The ghastly

Casey and his ghastly play will be silenced for good and the dead will respect us when night falls and the theatre is at last in darkness and his words have been erased forever.

*

ROBINSON Lady Gregory, the play is almost ready now. We have cut most of the song and I have written to O'Brien to assure him of that.

LADY GREGORY Yes, that's good. Give him a bone to gnaw on. I know we needed an RC on the board, but could we not have got someone who doesn't sniff as much and snivel as much?

ROBINSON He came recommended, your ladyship.

MISS CROWE I am here, your ladyship.

LADY GREGORY Miss Crowe, I understand that you and your friend Mr McCormick – who I also wished to see, but he is not in the building this morning – I believe that you are speaking to the other actors and to Mr Robinson about Casey.

MISS CROWE Some of the play, your ladyship –

LADY GREGORY The play is a masterpiece and you and all the other actors will speak every word unless I say or Mr Robinson says otherwise. You will not speak to anyone about the play except to Mr McCormick, and you will inform him what I have said and you will do so without comment. Have I made myself clear?

MISS CROWE Yes, ma'am.

MISS MOONEY Oh, Lady Gregory, there's going to be a great row. All the widows had a meeting: Madame Sheehy Skeffington, Madame MacBride and

Madame Pearse and Madame Kevin Barry and Madame Tom Clarke. That Madame Sheehy Skeffington, she's the fierce one, and they are going to put a stop to the play, or put a stop to all the money. Or they're going to march on us. And they have whistles. A riot!

LADY GREGORY And you are going to speak your lines like a good girl.

MISS MOONEY I am, your ladyship, I have them off by heart.

LADY GREGORY Let us hear them then.

MISS MOONEY 'You louse, you louse, you! ... You're no man ... You're no man ... I'm a woman, anyhow, an' if I'm a prostitute aself, I have me feelin's ... Thryin' to put his arm around me a minute ago, an' givin me th' glad eye, th' little wrigglin' lump o' desolation turns on me now, because he saw there was nothin' doin' ... You louse, you! If I was a man, or you were a woman, I'd bate th' puss o' you!'

*

YEATS Yes, this will cause very great offence. But they must not unfurl the flag. Having it there will be enough.

LADY GREGORY Now, you will not be heard against whistles.

YEATS I will write my statement in a clear hand ...

LADY GREGORY And clear spelling. Your spelling was not improved by the Nobel Prize.

YEATS And have it to the newspapers in time for the morning edition.

LADY GREGORY And you must deliver it personally. We have no idea now who is working for the other side.

And I shall go now. I have some trees to look after and my darling grandchildren to feed and it must not look like an ambush. Although it will be one.

*

YEATS [*to himself, declaiming*] You have made a great mistake. No, let me see … You are a disgraceful audience … no, no, again … You – yes this is right – have disgraced yourselves again. Is this to be an ever-recurring …

*

[*scene of* MISS MOONEY *showing her leg and the flag being waved*]

MISS MOONEY 'Dancin' a jig in th' bed, an' bawlin' for butther
an' bread.
An' there, to our joy, a bright bouncin' boy
Was dancin' a jig in th' bed!'

*

O'CASEY Yeats was like a cross between the President of the Executive Council running Ireland and Michael Collins running a guerrilla war. He does not rest. Not a poem is written during those weeks, and not a line from one of his terrible old plays. Instead, he hires men to carry sandwich-boards advertising the play, he speaks to them as though his own life depended on the message they carry. He spends a fortune on posters and puts big ads in the papers like it was

Clerys' sale. No one in Dublin is in any doubt but that there is something stirring in the Abbey Theatre. It is called *The Plough and the Stars* and it is electric. There are queues from early on for the cheap seats on the opening night and anyone who is anyone had tickets for the other seats.

And he stands receiving them all, his big head and his mane of hair, a bundle of raw power. I wouldn't have defied him that night if I were the King of England or Julius Caesar or the Kaiser himself. And they laugh when the lines are funny and they applaud when they are good and they cheer at the end. And that is Monday and I go on the stage and I bow. And I feel that lightness afterwards that I blame them for, the actors. I only want to be told I am great and they are great and it is great.

*

O'CASEY You were all great! It was a proud night. [*almost embraces* MCCORMICK, *who almost embraces him*] Eileen, I take it all back. You're the greatest woman from Rathmines there's ever been.

MISS CROWE Ah sure we knew you were only blackguarding. It's all forgotten now, although you shouldn't have written … [MCCORMICK *approaches and she is forced to withdraw.*]

MISS MOONEY They're all saying you're a great genius. Sure if they only knew you!

O'CASEY Maybe I'll say it to you later then.

MISS MOONEY Oh, you can say it to me now!

O'CASEY Well I will then.

MISS MOONEY Go on.

O'CASEY You saved the play, my play. If the people had disliked Rosie the other two acts would have failed. You made it real and you made them feel for her, like it could be one of themselves or their sisters, or maybe that's going a bit far, but you know what I mean. But they liked you enough not to judge her too much, and that was all I needed.

MISS MOONEY Maybe you'll put that in writing. I'm not sure it's a great compliment. Or maybe it is.

O'CASEY The next time I'll have you playing the Mother of God.

MISS MOONEY Go on now!

O'CASEY Ria, I wondered ...

MISS MOONEY What did you wonder?

O'CASEY It's dark these nights. I wondered if you needed someone to walk up the road with you.

MISS MOONEY You can wonder away, Johnny Cassidy. You'll walk nowhere with me. It's bad enough having to say your lines. You're the greatest –

O'CASEY Ah, come on, you will –

MISS MOONEY I will not!

*

O'CASEY It is a happy night, or reasonably happy, despite the snobby actresses. God, they were ungrateful after all I did for them! It's only when I am walking out, I realize that Yeats is still there. He hasn't gone near the Green Room. He is coming back from the gents to his office and it is only then I realize that we have not won the battle, that this is merely the placing of the forces on opposite hills and he knows this and no one else knows it. And he is ready, like a general. He barely speaks to me as he passes, but his gaze has none of that weird abstracted look he often puts on. His look is hard, like he is someone ready to take the prisoner out to be hanged with no further ado. He marches by me, and I know then that there will be more. It is strange how he knows that and none of the rest of us do.

The papers are good, cannot be better. Oh, it is a masterpiece and I am a genius, the usual stuff. I am tired of it. St Brigid remains in Coole. And Robinson gets drunk. All the usual things happen. There is a bit of hissing on the second night all right and then on the third we have to tell Shields not to unfurl the flag in the cheeky way he is doing it – he gets cheekier every night – because it is provoking them.

Yeats stays there night after night and is back again in the morning. He looks like a lion who has come into his prime. God, the clothes that Englishwoman gets for him, and the bow-ties, and the hair. He sees nobody for long and he speaks to nobody much at all. He grunts if you come near him. He is waiting and he is right. He is right all along.

On Thursday night, the widows attack the theatre. I haven't bothered coming in even and no one has a clue what is going to happen until oul' Larchet from the orchestra is told by some young fellow before Act II that if he values his instruments he should get them out of the way. They have it planned too and I wish I was there for the beginning of it because they are calling out for my blood.

*

VOICE [*from audience*] O'Casey out!

VOICE O'Casey the coward!

MAN'S VOICE [*from stage*] 'Bloodshed is a cleansing and sanctifying thing, and the nation that regards it as the final horror has lost its manhood … There are many things more horrible than bloodshed, and slavery is one of them!'

MISS MOONEY [*flag held by man beside her*] 'It's th' sacred thruth, mind you, what that man's afther sayin'.'

VOICE [*from audience*] There were no flags in the pubs.

VOICE There were no whores in the Rising.

VOICE O'Casey the coward!

VOICE Take the subsidy back. Pearse and Connolly are our heroes!

VOICE Brave men fought and died and now they're being mocked and maligned.

VOICE O'Casey the coward!

MISS MOONEY 'If y'ass Rosie, it's heartbreakin' to see a young fella thinkin' of anything, or admirin' anything, but silk thransparent stockin's showin' off the shape of a little lassie's legs!'

VOICE Get the flag off the stage!

[*Whistles in audience. Appearance of flag carried by men and* MISS MOONEY *and* MISS DELANY *with drinks, shouting lines, drowned out by whistles and catcalls … Appearance of* MRS SHEEHY SKEFFINGTON *marching silently, slowly, with dignity towards the stage.*]

O'CASEY [*aside*] It is like the beginning of the French Revolution. They storm the stage, attack all round them, squealing and shouting. I am too far back to get a few digs at them. God, it is marvellous to watch Fluther Good give a good fluthering dig in the jaw to some creepie crawlie and land him into the orchestra.

I move to the back to see if I can get around the side, so I can join in the fray, so I miss the bit where the coward McCormick tells them that the actors are just the mouthpieces and are not responsible for their lines. By the time I get close, they are becoming tired, but shouting and screaming nonetheless.

And then I see a sight to behold, something I will never forget. I see Yeats brushing past me, his hair combed back and paper in his hand. It is as though there are lights shining out of him and he rushes the stage, quicker and better than any of them ever did and he tries to speak.

YEATS [*being shouted down, whistles and voices*] You have disgraced yourselves again. Is this to be an ever-recurring celebration of Irish genius? Synge first, and then O'Casey. The news of the happenings of the past few minutes will go from country to country. Dublin has once more rocked the cradle of genius. From such a scene in this theatre went forth the fame of Synge.

Equally the fame of O'Casey is born here tonight. This is his apotheosis.

O'CASEY [*aside*] Apotheosis all right! The last time I saw my apotheosis it was under the bed waiting to be emptied.

*

GARDA GILHOOLEY Come on now, missus.

MRS SHEEHY SKEFFINGTON Do not manhandle me! I wish to make it clear that I am being escorted from this theatre because I have made a protest on behalf of truth against the mocking of the dead, on behalf of decent and brave men whose memory is being dragged in the mud, while the looters and the shirkers are being exalted.

GARDA MORONEY Easy now, ma'am, and it's a lovely night outside.

MAUD GONNE MacBRIDE Get your filthy hands off me, you Free State scoundrel.

MORONEY You take her, Mick, and I'll drag the other one.

MRS SHEEHY SKEFFINGTON Do not manhandle me!

MAUD GONNE MacBRIDE Take your Free State hands off the brave people who died for Ireland.

GILHOOLEY [*doubling over in pain*] Oh Christ Almighty! She's after … she's after destroying me. I'll be … oh God, when I get home …

*

O'CASEY It's only in the morning I realize what Yeats has done and where he went before he rushed the stage. He slipped out himself to the newspapers with copies of his statement so that he didn't need to be heard. The whole country heard him in the morning. It made the headlines. He had it all ready. And the next day too St Brigid of Coole comes up on the train and he meets her at the station. It is the first time I have ever seen poor Lady Gregory tired. She has been up before the dawn to catch the early train, and the riots have not excited her as they have excited Yeats. Instead, they have drained some of the life out of her.

*

LADY GREGORY How do you think we will be viewed in the future? Do you think it will matter what we have done?

YEATS This building has been an ark against reason, a place where the imagination can take shelter. This will always matter, even if it matters only to the few.

LADY GREGORY Is it possible that we did only damage?

YEATS What? You and I? Damage?

LADY GREGORY Our class, our race. In the whole of our history, what have we done? A few stray houses and gardens and castles and the language they never needed. And all the cruelty.

YEATS You and I have soared above class and race. These are things which have nothing to do with us. At the times when we are searching for the right word, the right line, we have no class and we belong to no race. The cruelty has not been ours.

LADY GREGORY I believed when I left here to go to Coole that we would win this battle, but now I know we have lost. Soon, they will ban our books and trample on our freedom. The rioters have won. The censor will be lord. O'Brien and his like have won. It does not look like that now, but for the future I see only darkness.

YEATS We belong in the dark; we will go back there. In the meantime, I love the redness of life battling against the black night.

LADY GREGORY We have lost. We have left nothing.

YEATS We have created beauty in a broken place, beautiful words when there were only slogans, images that pierce the soul in an age when the belittling noise, the boast and the curse reigned in the streets. It was done for its own sake.

LADY GREGORY I need you to answer me now if it has mattered what we have done, if we will leave behind nothing but a few play-scripts ... I need to know.

YEATS You mean ...

LADY GREGORY I mean intellectual freedom rooted somewhere in the mind of this country, the freedom that must come before everything.

YEATS As long as there is one mind alive –

LADY GREGORY No, I don't mean one mind. I mean the country, I mean the society, the new state.

YEATS A piercing shriek, a folding wave, a flutter of wings mean more to me than governments or society or the state.

LADY GREGORY You have hardly left the building since the play opened.

YEATS I shall use every trick I know so that Casey shall be heard.

LADY GREGORY Was it right to call the police?

YEATS When I called the police I took pleasure in knowing that it was their own police came to quieten them and escort them to the street. And I am ready to press charges in their own courts. And I wish to have a great debate as we did with the *Playboy*, flush them out, let them make the case for foolishness and for the rule of the rabble and we will argue for freedom and for noble art and for Ireland.

LADY GREGORY No, I have considered this matter and there will be no debate in this theatre. I have come from Coole to advise you not to attempt it.

YEATS The last time, we routed them in the debate over the *Playboy*.

LADY GREGORY The last time it was a battle between those of us who use a toothbrush and the others who don't. But this time it is different.

YEATS I notice no difference, they had the same greenish stains on their teeth, the protestors I saw, and the same foul breath.

LADY GREGORY This time there are women involved. And I have a policy never to have a debate of any sort with a woman. Especially not an argument with a group of widows. Just when you have completed your argument, they weep.

YEATS What shall we do then?

LADY GREGORY It is why I wonder what our legacy will be, that there are young men and women out there who risked everything for Ireland, and still they do not believe that Casey's right to speak comes before their right to silence him. What have we achieved if that is not understood?

The problem also lies in the nature of the enemy. We are arguing against grief, against the lines that run between hurt and pride. These women want their men back. Those who have given up wanting them by day want them more fiercely when night falls. They wake in the night, going over and over how the news came and how it might have been otherwise; they long for more innocent times, and they cannot admit they have such longings, for the child back in their arms, or the young man's first embrace or his return to them. They must be proud instead of hurt. That is who we are up against. We will call the police again if we have to, but we will press no charges. We will silence them only because we have to, but we will go no further.

⋆

FIRST WOMAN Let me go. You're worse than the peelers. You're squeezing my arm. Oh Jesus, Mary and Joseph, I'm being tortured.

GILHOOLEY Keep your hands off me now!

SECOND WOMAN You're only a coward. You're an RIC man.

MORONEY If you don't follow me now, I'll give you RIC.

SECOND WOMAN Oh holy, he has me by the coat. You're tearing me coat.

GILHOOLEY You'll have charges pressed.

FIRST WOMAN [*sings*] 'God save Ireland say the heroes / God save Ireland say we all ...'

SECOND WOMAN [*sings*] 'A rebel hand set the heather blazing / And brought the neighbours from far and near ... And then Father ...'

MORONEY Out with the two of you now. You're a disgrace to Ireland!

FIRST WOMAN Maud Gonne was well able for you!

SECOND WOMAN Maud put the fear of God into you!

*

O'CASEY In those days there was something about her which reminded me of my mother in her last years, tired and sad and easy to irritate, but watching out, always watching out. She was like a great god in the last days of the gods. She ran the building and all who sailed in her, but she left statements in the press unchallenged. She wanted me to toe the line. No letters to the papers. No debate. If she and Nine Bean Rows thought that I was going to sit in my flat or walk the streets of Dublin and be insulted, they were wrong. I'll write what letters I like. So I crossed swords with Mrs Sheehy Skeffington in the *Irish Independent*. I was ready to argue with her and win. I would take no orders from anyone. It was time we attacked our enemies with what we knew best. Words.

*

MRS SHEEHY SKEFFINGTON How is your arthritis, Mr O'Brien?

O'BRIEN Between the damp weather and having to listen to W.B. Yeats on the subject of liberty, it is not great. Yeats is a great burden to his friends and acquaintances alike, [*to* MAUD GONNE MacBRIDE] saving your presence.

MAUD GONNE MacBRIDE Oh, don't apologize to me. I knew Willie Yeats before any of them, of course. He was all the fashion then – everyone wanted to marry him. I was alone, I think, in not quite seeing the point of him.

O'BRIEN Yes, yes. He's well married now, anyway.

MRS SHEEHY SKEFFINGTON Well, Lady Gregory and his wife can keep him in England and O'Casey too. They can put their plays on there.

MAUD GONNE MacBRIDE You know, she wrote that play.

MRS SHEEHY SKEFFINGTON What play?

MAUD GONNE MacBRIDE Lady Gregory wrote *Cathleen Ni Houlihan*.

O'BRIEN *Who* wrote it?

MAUD GONNE MacBRIDE Lady Gregory wrote that play. But he took it from her.

MRS SHEEHY SKEFFINGTON Are you sure?

MAUD GONNE MacBRIDE It was his idea and he wrote the chant at the end, but the rest is her work and her work alone. I should know, I played the part. You know, he was always tremendously bored by the middle of plays, his own have only beginnings and endings. It was her work.

O'BRIEN Are you sure that she did not merely type it?

MAUD GONNE MacBRIDE No, I am certain that Lady Gregory wrote it. It is hers alone except for the ending. Of course, she fled to Italy as soon as *Cathleen Ni Houlihan* went on and she saw the power it had. And Yeats soon fled to London, where he always fled. They are, I have to say, a most dreadful pair.

O'BRIEN Yes, yes. The meetings with them are excruciating. They'd put years on you. Ladies, we'll have to find a way out of this difficult situation.

MRS SHEEHY SKEFFINGTON The way out is simple, Mr O'Brien. Put on another play, one of Lady Gregory's comedies, for example, or *The Shaughraun*, and drop this one. Cowards and fallen women and a drunken rabble consorting with the men who died, as though they were somehow the heroes! Mr O'Brien, I knew the heroes, I was there, I knew all of them, my own husband died, as Madame MacBride's husband died.

MAUD GONNE MacBRIDE And Mrs Sheehy Skeffington was handled most roughly by the Free State police. Have we achieved nothing after our long struggle that Irish police could manhandle the widow of Francis Sheehy Skeffington? Is that what it has come to? Perhaps you could tell the lord and lady of Abbey Street that it is they who have disgraced themselves again. Ireland now belongs to the Irish people. Tell them the British have left and it is time they left too, taking their cowardly playwright with them.

O'BRIEN Ladies, if we could suspend the protests, perhaps we could find a compromise. I think the government will have a ready answer for everybody because this sort of codology can't go on, and there are books and films and …

MRS SHEEHY SKEFFINGTON You mean censorship?

O'BRIEN Yes, yes. Action. Legislation. Yes, yes. That'll be next. I know O'Casey is a communist, or he was before this writing lark started. An agitator. And no respect for religion or for his betters or for anything. I don't know where they got him from. But it is my experience that people like him always end up in England. Plenty of work over there. I don't think we'll be hearing much more from him. Let him fizzle out, is my view. Attacking him is only encouraging him. God, he's caused us nothing but trouble! But the directors would love to find a compromise.

MRS SHEEHY SKEFFINGTON Mr O'Brien, you should tell them that they are not dealing with the *Playboy* rioters, that they are dealing with me and people like me, who will not give in so easily.

O'BRIEN Yes, yes.

*

MISS RICHARDS 'Look, Jack, look at th' anger in his face; look at th' fear glintin' in his eyes ... He himself's afraid, afraid, afraid! ... He wants you to go th' way he'll have th' chance of death sthrikin' you an' missin' him! ... Turn round an' look at him, Jack, look at him, look at him! ... His very soul is cold ... shiverin' with th' thought of what may happen to him ... It is his fear that is thryin' to frighten you from recognizin' th' same fear that is in your own heart!'

*

LADY GREGORY Now, Miss Mooney, stand up straight. This is

your costume and I don't wish you to wear any other. Your legs … Cover them!

MISS MOONEY They're covered, your ladyship.

LADY GREGORY Now what are your legs for? Why did the good Lord give you two legs?

MISS MOONEY To help me stand up, your ladyship.

LADY GREGORY Is there any mention in the Bible, or in any other book, of your legs being a prominent aspect of your brazenness?

MISS MOONEY Do you mean me? Oh God now!

LADY GREGORY Miss Mooney, what you do outside this theatre is none of my concern. But night after night now you are flaunting yourself on this stage in a way that is entirely unnecessary. You are personally causing decent people to join the riots when we have trouble enough.

MISS MOONEY But I am playing a prostitute, your ladyship.

LADY GREGORY Who is in a public house and off duty, so to speak. You will say out your lines and cease to flaunt yourself. Now could I have the young man who waves the flag.

MR SHIELDS I am here, your ladyship.

LADY GREGORY So you are. I thought it was you. Who told you to unfurl the flag?

SHIELDS No one, your ladyship.

LADY GREGORY Then get out of my sight and if you unfurl that flag once more, I shall have plenty more to say to you. Now where is McCormick?

McCORMICK Here, your ladyship.

LADY GREGORY I understand that you do not like Sean O'Casey.

McCORMICK Yes.

LADY GREGORY Yes, what?

McCORMICK Yes, your ladyship.

LADY GREGORY Do you dislike Mr Sean O'Casey?

McCORMICK I do, your ladyship.

LADY GREGORY Are you an actor, are you, are you?

McCORMICK Yes, your ladyship.

LADY GREGORY No one can hear you.

McCORMICK Yes, your ladyship.

LADY GREGORY You are mumbling and muttering the lines night after night. Are there groups of the unemployed gathered daily in the streets?

McCORMICK Yes, your ladyship.

LADY GREGORY And boats to Liverpool thronged with young Irishmen looking for work?

McCORMICK Yes, your ladyship.

LADY GREGORY You shall join them if you mutter one more of this great playwright's lines. Am I understood?

McCORMICK Yes, your ladyship.

LADY GREGORY Louder!

McCORMICK Yes, your ladyship.

LADY GREGORY We want to hear you at the back of the hall.

McCORMICK You will, your ladyship.

*

LADY GREGORY So sweet the actors. I have had a few soft words with them ... So talented!

YEATS So I heard.

LADY GREGORY And I have spoken severely to Robinson, who was in the bar during last night's performance.

YEATS Unfortunately, O'Brien attended last night's performance too, and I think we may have left him waiting outside for long enough.

LADY GREGORY Yes, twenty-five minutes was what I had in mind.

Doctors recommend it as the best cooling-off period for board members who have been consorting with the other side. Could you ask him to come in?

O'BRIEN [*limping*] Yes, yes. I think, as members of the board, we should be fully aware that there are threats being made against this theatre.

YEATS Yes, they are being made nightly by some of the audience, and we are dealing with them forcefully and, I think, rather well.

O'BRIEN There are threats being made of a more serious sort. To not only the theatre but the people who work here, including the directors.

LADY GREGORY That is nothing new. During the Troubles, Mr O'Brien, I was threatened by one of my tenants and I told him as I tell you now that I do not heed threats.

O'BRIEN In the performance last evening, I noticed some of the actors flaunting themselves, almost inviting a riot. I know it is a difficult time for them but –

YEATS We have noted their antics and they will cease.

O'BRIEN Mrs Sheehy Skeffington has written to the *Irish Independent* setting out her views, and I have had informal contacts from the government and I can say that members of the cabinet are concerned about the play. It is a difficult time for the cabinet and –

YEATS That is all as it should be. If Mrs Sheehy Skeffington appears screaming in this theatre once more, I shall press charges against her. As far as the government is concerned, it is their job to govern the country, as it is ours to run the theatre.

O'BRIEN Unfortunately, the theatre is part of the country.

YEATS It is the best part of the country. And that is because of its independence. It is free of all interference as gold is free of dull rock, and it will remain so, whether your contacts with the government remain formal, informal or, even better, non-existent.

O'BRIEN We cannot ask for total independence and then expect a subsidy.

LADY GREGORY Mr O'Brien, we merely ask for the subsidy – they are free to refuse, but we expect our independence. Indeed, we demand it!

O'BRIEN Yes, yes. The play has caused nothing but bitterness.

YEATS No, for those who have heard it, it has caused an uplift in their spirits. The city, without *The Plough and the Stars* playing nightly, is a drab and dull place, as indeed the riots and the rioters themselves are dull, like a carthorse who has pulled free of the cart: mindless, pointless, disruptive, irritating, but easy to quell. The city without *The Plough and the Stars* is an unimaginable place, nothing more than a feudal grouping, a shapeless and ugly mass.

LADY GREGORY Mr O'Brien, I say to the rioters and to the government what I said to the representative of the Lord Lieutenant when he asked me at the time of *Blanco Posnet* if there was no way out. I said there was none, except our being left alone, and I say that again. We must be left alone.

O'BRIEN Yes, yes.

*

MISS RICHARDS 'I can't help thinkin' every shot fired 'll be fired at Jack, an' every shot fired at Jack'll be fired at me. What do I care for th' others? I can think only of me own self … An' there's no woman gives a son or a husband to be killed – if they say it, they're lyin', lyin', against God, Nature, an' against themselves! … One blasted hussy at a barricade told me to go home an' not be thryin' to dishearten th' men … That I wasn't worthy to bear a son to a man that was out fightin' for freedom … I clawed at her, an' smashed her in th' face till we were separated … I was pushed down th' street, an' I cursed them – cursed the rebel ruffians an' Volunteers that had dhragged me ravin' mad into th' sthreets to seek me husband!'

*

O'CASEY Goodnight, men. Is there a play on, is there?

MORONEY [*whistling 'Nora'*] Oh now.

GILHOOLEY [*whistling*] Oh now.

O'CASEY Is there good dancers in the play? I mean good –

GILHOOLEY If you want dancing now –

MORONEY There's more than dancing.

O'CASEY English dancers?

GILHOOLEY Will you go away. English? They are our girls. Nice Irish girls and they have to say lines that wouldn't get in to Dantey's *Inferno*.

MORONEY Oh, lines! The fellow who wrote it is a communist and he would be refused the sacraments only he is a Protestant. And Maud Gonne is going to take action against him and she's the one. Isn't she, Mick?

GILHOOLEY Oh God, she's a terror. Mrs Sheehy Skeffington is a lady, a real lady, but the Gonne woman is a terror.

O'CASEY Why is that?

MORONEY Oh now!

GILHOOLEY The less said now.

MORONEY Sure we had to drag her out screaming from the play and the curses off her. You'd need double pay for that one. Ah but I couldn't tell you the rest.

GILHOOLEY Treble pay. And an early pension.

MORONEY She caught Guard Gilhooley by his private parts.

GILHOOLEY It was gentle as a breeze first when it started.

MORONEY But then it grew tighter, didn't it, Mick, until, when he lifted her off the ground, she began to squeeze.

GILHOOLEY She has the grip of a docker round his first pint after a hard day's loading. She has one big strong fist on her.

MORONEY And she wouldn't let go.

GILHOOLEY Until, as she squeezed away, I saw both the plough and the stars. Until I couldn't tell which was which.

MORONEY Sure, he could be heard in the Comeragh Mountains.

O'CASEY Is she in tonight, Maud Gonne?

GILHOOLEY If I see her again ...

MORONEY No, they're keeping the powder dry for the

meeting tomorrow night.

GILHOOLEY She's at home practising. That what she's doing. But do you know something? There's a girl on that stage …

MORONEY There is …

GILHOOLEY A girl.

MORONEY We call her Nora.

GILHOOLEY Because she plays the part of Nora.

MORONEY She's our girl. We like them all, but we like her the best. We are meant to go in when the riots start, but often we go in just to hear Nora. Oh she's a gorgeous girl. Sure we know all her lines.

GILHOOLEY 'And you liked your new hat; didn't you, didn't you?'

MORONEY 'Jack, Jack; please, Jack! I thought you were tired of that sort of thing long ago.'

[*both* GARDAÍ *remain still, guarding the theatre, serious, as they speak these lines*]

MORONEY 'Oh, yes, your little, little red-lipped Nora's a sweet little girl when th' fit seizes you; but your little, little red-lipped Nora has to clean your boots every mornin', all the same.'

GILHOOLEY 'Oh, well, if we're goin' to be snotty!' God, imagine using that word to Nora? Isn't that terrible.

MORONEY And then they make her say it. 'Snotty!' she shouts out. God, it must break her heart. She's a lovely girl and it's a disgrace what's happening in there every night.

GILHOOLEY And tax payers' money.

[*sound of riots inside*]

MORONEY God almighty, they're after sneaking in again on us tonight. If that Maud Gonne is there ...

GILHOOLEY And all the fault of that scut of a playwright. Casey! God, if I ever lay eyes on him, I'll put on a personal baton charge.

MORONEY God, I hope they're not hurting Nora. Come on quick!

*

O'CASEY They wanted to have a great debate, the widows and their acolytes, and wanted a big evening in Mills Hall with the crowd hanging from the rafters, theatre-lovers all, where they could insult me in person and my play by proxy. They all wrote to the papers in advance saying that I had glorified fear and cowardice, and then they wrote saying that the flag had never been taken into a pub. I wrote back and told them in cold print that I had seen it there myself. The Green White and Gold has appeared in strange places, I told them. I saw it painted on a lavatory in the Gloucester Diamond, and I told them that; and I saw it thrust out of the window of a famous old shebeen, and I added that for luck; and I ended by telling them that for their information it was also made to function as a state robe for the Mayor of Waterford, a burly gentleman of the old school, with underdeveloped manners and a bad case of the dandruff.

And just to put the wind up them, craw-thumpers one and all, I quoted from the Good Book to them, the book they are all meant to abide by, but are not allowed to read. I quoted from the Book of Job: 'Upon the earth there is not his like, who is made without fear.'

I was ready for the widows all the next night I was. I would have the Bible in my head and right on my side, even if Yeats and St Brigid refused to belittle themselves by appearing at the meeting in the hall. They had better things to do, they said, sitting in the bee-loud glade of the Abbey Theatre watching mad oul' wans, and their skinny brothers and sons who were under the bed in 1916 and every other day too, being hauled out of the theatre for shouting abuse at a crowd of actors. So I went along on my own, ready for the fray, like Cuchulain of old, except that my eyes were hurting me and I had words at will and I had a play running in the West End of London and another at the Abbey Theatre, which is more than Cuchulain ever did.

*

MRS SHEEHY SKEFFINGTON I have come here this evening to speak about a matter which I believe is foremost in our culture and in the new Ireland we have all been working for. It is an easy matter to define and thus it is something which is also easy to destroy and make little of. It is the most important thing we have, it is our most treasured possession, it belongs to us communally and as individuals. Put simply: it is how we remember. And how we remember defines more than anything else who we are and who we will be.

I wish to make clear that our demonstration against *The Plough and the Stars* was not directed against any individual actor, nor was it directed to the moral aspect of the play. It was solely on national grounds. We wished to voice a passionate indignation against the outrage of a drama staged in a supposedly national theatre which held the men and women of Easter Week up to derision and obloquy. There is a point beyond which toleration becomes merely servility, and the sort of realism which the work displays is not art but morbid perversity. In no country save in Ireland could a state-subsidized theatre presume on popular patience to the extent of making a mockery of a revolutionary movement on which our present society was built.

I am one of those who have gone for over twenty years to performances at the Abbey, and I admire as no other the earlier ideals of the theatre that produced *Cathleen Ni Houlihan*, which sent Seán Connolly, to name but one, and I name him as a dear friend, out to his death on Easter Week. This same Abbey, built on high ideals and immense talent and hard work, that helped to make Easter Week, is now in its subsidized, sleek old age, ready to jeer and sneer at its former enthusiasms.

O'CASEY [*aside*] I was waiting for her to name her own husband killed in the fighting, but she did not. They couldn't take their eyes off her, whatever she found in herself that night. I had never seen her talk before. In her voice came something strange for me, a real voice appeared, or maybe not real if you studied it, or held back from it. And she was wrong, I'll have to say that. But that wasn't what mattered. Something else mattered. She meant what she said and she had nothing to gain and I forgot my eyes, which had stung all that week, and I forgot my hatred for her. I just looked at her, and listened, and that's what everyone else in the hall did too.

MRS SHEEHY SKEFFINGTON

The only censorship that is justified is the free censorship of popular opinion. The Ireland which remembers with tear-dimmed eyes all that Easter Week stands for will not and cannot be silent in the face of this challenge.

A play in which every character connected with the Citizen Army is a coward, a slacker or worse, that omits no detail of squalid slumdom, the looting, the squabbling, the disease and degeneracy, yet that omits any revelation of the glory and the inspiration of Easter Week, is a *Hamlet* shown without the Prince of Denmark. Is it merely a coincidence that the only soldiers whose knees do not knock together and who are not indifferent to the glories of their uniforms are the British Army?

I learn that Mr O'Casey's personal knowledge of the Citizen Army does not extend beyond 1914 and 1915. To those, however, who remember the men and women of 1916, such presentation is a gross libel and a stain on our memory. The women of Easter Week were not like Nora Clitheroe, just as her futile, snivelling husband is not typical of Irish manhood. The women of Easter, as we know them, are typified rather in the mother of Patrick Pearse, that valiant woman who gave both of her sons for freedom. They shall be remembered forever, while the garrison mentality in the Abbey Theatre, which calls the police nightly, will be soon forgotten.

O'CASEY [*aside*] They rose to cheer and as they did I saw faces I didn't know were there that night. I saw Liam O'Flaherty, the so-called revolutionary and nature-lover, baying for my blood, and I saw Austin Clarke, who couldn't rhyme his way out of a wet paper bag, loving it, standing to cheer that the play should be taken off. They were ready to join the ignorant mob, led as ignorant mobs are, and always will be, by a brave woman who spoke her mind.

All the hurt was in every line she said. I liked her husband, the little I knew of him, and I liked her too that night, and now it was my turn and I was ready for them because I hated every one of them when I stood up and looked at them. I was ready to tell them that Nora Clitheroe represented the feeling of womanhood everywhere, not only Ireland's women, but the women of the human race. The safety of her brood is the true mark of every woman and the true morality. A mother does not like her son to be killed, nor a woman her husband.

I was ready to tell them about tear-dimmed eyes and they shall be remembered forever. Some of the men who fought could not even get a job. Will that be remembered?

Oh, but something happened. I wish I could say that it was the thought that I would, if I came to England, never have to lay eyes on one of these people again, the Maud Gonnes and the Clarkes and the O'Flahertys, that I could go; I wish I could say that I did not need to speak. There is no explanation I can think of for sitting down instead of starting. I suppose I had written the play and that was my defence. But I didn't think that either.

I was weary and my head was buzzing. I had listened to her too carefully, I had sort of followed her too closely so that I could see … not what she thought, or that she was right … but that her voice was the great voice, her hurt the oldest one and … oh I sat down, I don't know why I sat down.

After a few others spoke, I tried again but I was no use, and what I remember more than anything else about the rest of that night was Mrs Sheehy Skeffington's bravery when everyone kept away from me like I was Moby Dick and had landed in the docks, or was Rosie Redmond herself come to meet her old clients who were out for a walk on Sunday with their respectable wives. She moved towards me and she shook my hand and she had tears in her eyes when she told me that she had just read my book on the Citizen Army and what I said about her husband who was a good man. She held my right hand with her two hands. And I felt then that whatever she thought and whatever I wrote, it was the women left after that Rising who suffered the most and she was one of them and their memory was precious just as their fear and their love had once merged into a terror and a grief which were written into every word they spoke and breath they managed and every line on their faces. The two of us looked at each other for a few seconds as we recognized that fact in all its … and then she turned away and I went home.

*

BARMAN [*wiping counter*] 'Nothin' much doin' in your line tonight, Rosie?'

MISS MOONEY 'Curse o' God on th' haporth, hardly, Tom. There isn't much notice taken of a pretty petticoat of a night like this … They're all in a holy mood. Th' solemn-lookin' dials on th' whole o' them an' they marchin' to th' meetin'. You'd think they were th' glorious company of th' saints, an' th' noble army of martyrs thrampin' through th' streets of paradise. They're all thinkin' of higher things than a girl's garthers …'

VOICE Get her off the stage!

MISS MOONEY [*showing her leg*] 'It's a tremendous meetin'; four platforms they have – there's one o' them just outside opposite th' window.'

VOICE There were no streetwalkers in the Rising!

BARMAN 'Oh, ay; sure when th' speaker comes [*motioning with his hand*] to th' near end, here, you can see him plain, an' hear nearly everythin' he's spoutin' out of him.'

VOICE Pearse died for Ireland!

MISS MOONEY 'It's no joke thryin' to make up fifty-five shillin's a week for your keep an' laundhry, an' then taxin' you a quid for your own room if you bring home a friend for th' night … If I could only put by a couple of quid for a swankier outfit, everythin' in th' garden ud look lovely –'

VOICE O'Casey, get the boat to England!

BARMAN 'Whisht, till we hear what he's sayin'.'

*

O'CASEY It struck me on one of those nights what it might have been like if the English had never set foot in Ireland. I looked at the ugliness all around me, them all howling. I suppose they would have gone on making stone crosses and gathered at holy wells and having fist-fights and faction fights while the senile monks in the monasteries sat quietly writing out their old stories, making heroes out of idiots, half-savages locked into darkness. And they were still locked into darkness. In their minds they hadn't moved from the time when they lived in holes in the ground. I could see it in their faces. Oh, they loved heroes and martyrs, but after the event. Most of them wouldn't join the Vincent de Paul they were so cautious. And the green snots coming out of their nostrils all winter long.

God, I was glad to get away from them. Ireland. Full of preachers and screechers.

Yeats knew about power, I don't know where he learned about it, the power of a line of a poem, the power of a building, the power of the police. I never liked him, but I'll say that for him. And she … she knew everything, she must have dreamed about her dead son, her only child, shot down in the war, and how the news came and how she wished … She knew how to make peace and she knew how to stand firm. I should have made it up with her and she's dead now. She would have loved to see me happy, which is more than I can say for the rest of them.

Still, after *The Plough and the Stars* had its run and before we fell out, we had a few good years and maybe that is what I should think about now that she is gone. In London before the row I saw her every time she came; she was Lady Gregory fresh from her Irish estates and they got a chair for her, but I was a lord too, Lord Johnny Cassidy of Dorset Street, pointed out everywhere I went, and we made a great couple. She was proud of me and I was proud of myself. In Mayfair and Piccadilly, away from the sly looks they gave you in their great Free State.

On one of those nights as we walked through the bright streets of the greatest city in the world, she asked me, like she was a youngster starting to write, what was it, what was a play for me, how did I do it? And we stopped somewhere, on a corner like we were waiting for someone else, and I didn't know that I was really meant to answer until she asked me again. And I told her that there was a light in all of us, a little light, a sort of glimmer, and if you could work hard enough and if the time was right, you could get it onto a page, the words like faint stars, half-there, until you worked on them more. The plays were like glitter, I said, and they needed enough darkness so they could shine out and sparkle, but they needed brightness too, just enough, to reflect against.

We stood there on the side of the street in the strange city, the traffic roaring by, and people we didn't know and we'd never know passing us, a lord and a lady, and I told her, and I meant it, that it was I who made the glitter, but it was she and Nine Bean Rows, when the others tried to stop me, used all their power to make sure that there was enough light and enough shadow for the glitter to stand out and to matter, so that it could be seen by everyone who wanted to see it, and even by some who didn't, and could live on for a while even if we grew old, or fell out with each other, or became part of the night ourselves, the great mystery that is beyond us. She nodded and said nothing and we walked on as far as we could, we walked on, we walked on.